LEAD
TO
SUCCEED

10 Traits of Great Leadership in Business and Life

ALSO BY RICK PITINO

Born to Coach
Full-Court Pressure
Success Is a Choice

LEAD TO SUCCEED

10 Traits of Great Leadership in Business and Life

RICK PITINO
with Bill Reynolds

Broadway Books

NEW YORK

BROADWAY

A hardcover edition of this book was published in 2000 by Broadway Books.

Broadway Books titles may be purchased for business or promotional use or for
special sales. For information, please write to: Special Markets Department,
Random House, Inc., 1540 Broadway, New York, NY 10036.

BROADWAY BOOKS and its logo, a letter B bisected on the diagonal, are
trademarks of Broadway Books, a division of Random House, Inc.

The Library of Congress has cataloged the hardcover edition as follows:

Pitino, Rick.
   Lead to succeed: 10 traits of great leadership in business and life / Rick
Pitino with Bill Reynolds.
       p. cm.
       1. Leadership. 2. Success in business. 3. Success. I. Reynolds, Bill, 1945–
II. Title.

HD57.7 .P575 2000
658.4'092—dc21

                                                                    00-027196

Visit our website at www.broadwaybooks.com

First trade paperback edition published 2001.

Designed by Robert Bull Design

ISBN 0-7679-0342-0

10 9 8 7 6 5 4 3

To all the athletes I coached through all the years who had the desire to reach their potential.

And to my mom, who has always gone beyond the call of duty to help her children.

—RICK PITINO

Contents

Acknowledgments

David Vigliano, who first brought us together on a book thirteen years ago, continues to be the all-star of literary agents. Suzanne Oaks is as good as it gets as an editor, and her vision for the book was always there. Without her, this would be a different book and nowhere near as good.

They both have our enduring thanks.

As does Tom Wallace for his research, and help.

Introduction:
LEARNING TO BE A LEADER

When I was twenty-four years old I was selected to be the basketball coach at Boston University, becoming at that time one of the youngest head coaches in the country. I was thrilled to be picked for that top spot, but the unmitigated euphoria of getting the job quickly ended. I looked around at these players who were now looking at *me* for all the answers. I realized that I had to be a leader.

But how?

Leaders are not born, I believe, or at least I felt that I had not been born to be one. Nor was there any weekend seminar I could attend, or any course I could take, at least none that I was aware of at the time. There was not a pill I could swallow that overnight was going to turn me into an enlightened leader, some magic potion to quickly give me all the right answers. I had to learn how to be a leader by trial and error, by figuring out what worked for me and what didn't. There's no doubt I made my share of mistakes along the way. Gradually, though, by observing others who were in leadership positions, by seeing what worked and what didn't, I began to learn how to become an effective leader myself.

Ever since those early coaching years, I have been fascinated with the nature of leadership and its role in organizations.

What is the essence of great leadership?

Why are some people able to get other people to follow them, while other people don't seem to have this ability? Why are some people able to get other people to not only achieve their potential, but even move beyond it? Why are some people able to get others to achieve great things, while others cannot do this? Why do some companies grow, while others with just as much potential flounder, never seeing that potential actualized?

These are some key questions I asked myself as I studied leaders in all walks of life. And as I began to understand the reasons why certain people were effective leaders, and the traits they shared, this awareness eventually led to other more significant questions:

Are there certain traits of leadership that can be taught? If so, what are they?

Can anyone learn to be a more effective leader? If so, how?

These questions may have never been so important as they are today. From politics to business, and from education to coaching, the concept of leadership is under a national microscope. Companies are merging, streamlining, trying to position themselves for a future that seems to be changing by the week. Everyone in business today is under pressure to cut costs, improve the quality of goods and services, try to stay ahead of the competition and the technology curve, and do what they do better, all within a climate of uncertainty. The business climate changes rapidly, and while no one knows where the future is going to take us, we all know that it's going to be somewhere different.

With so many aspects of our work and personal lives up in the air, we need leadership more than ever as we head into a new century. Good leaders provide a vision. Good leaders take away the doubt and uncertainty, the fear of the future. Good leaders provide an environment in which other people can grow. Good leaders instill values. Good leaders make the people around them more successful.

There is little mystery to this. Successful organizations don't just happen, suddenly appearing in some puff of smoke. They don't happen by accident. Nor do they happen in a vacuum.

They happen because of strong leadership, some vision that's able to be actualized.

This always has been true, as timeless as leadership itself, but the entire concept of leadership has become muddled and confused. This is especially true in this era where traditional roles have been questioned, where the entire concept of authority is different from what it was a generation ago.

We now see, in politics and business, leaders who cannot lead themselves trying to lead others. We see people trying to lead by being friends with the people they are leading, and then wondering why it doesn't work. We see people in leadership situations in the workplace who possess few, if any, leadership skills, and then we wonder why both production and morale in that particular workplace is so low. We see people fail all the time as leaders and bring down organizations with them, affecting other people's lives. We see companies that start out with great potential, only to hit some invisible plateau, seemingly unable to move forward. We see people fail simply because they don't possess the tools—or understand the traits—it takes to be successful as leaders. Simply having the title doesn't make you a leader. This is what I had to learn back when I was a young coach, just starting out in my chosen profession. It's an important lesson, maybe *the* most important lesson. People are placed in leadership positions and think that simply having the title makes them effective leaders, that simply by being called "the boss" solves all the problems and makes everything function both smoothly and efficiently. It does not. Not even close. Leaders are only effective when they effectively lead the people of whom they're in charge. More to the point, leaders are only successful when the people they're leading become successful.

Sounds simple, right?

Yet this is overlooked time and time again. People are placed all the time in positions of leadership—whether it's in business, education, sports, whatever—and told, "Good luck." They are given a pat on the back and sent on their way. They are sent to lead others on little more than a wing and a prayer. No matter that they're ignorant of many of the skills needed to be effective leaders or that they immediately make time-honored mistakes, for the simple reason that no one gives them any alternatives. No matter that they're ill-prepared to be leaders and have about as much chance to be successful as they do in winning the lottery.

Some, of course, eventually learn on their own through trial and error and become effective leaders. Some never do, will forever seem as if they're working on intricate puzzles they can never solve, forever walking on some treadmill to failure.

* * *

I can spot a poor leader a mile away.

They're the people who are giving in all the time, the people who operate with a lack of discipline. As soon as I hear the expression "He's a player's coach," or "He's a boss whom everyone likes," I know that eventually, the discipline is going to break down; it's just a matter of time. When you lack discipline—be it in an office or on a basketball team—your chances for success have been significantly narrowed.

Discipline is your foundation: You have to have it, the people you are leading have to have it, the group has to have it. Discipline—showing up, putting in the effort, taking responsibility for your actions—sets the tone for all the work you do. Without it, all your great intentions will soon begin to unravel, and your vision cannot be actualized. Without discipline, your game plan will start to become unglued the first time you are severely tested.

I can put up with many things from the people who work for me, whether it's immaturity, poor fundamentals, bad techniques, lack of focus, or any of the laundry list of negatives that are out there. But I will not put up with a lack of effort. As a leader, I cannot tolerate that. The other negatives can be improved upon, changed, but a lack of effort undermines everything that you have worked for, and that is why a leader must maintain good discipline among those he or she leads.

It's discipline that gets you through adversity and discipline that is the very foundation of your goals and your mission statement as an organization. In short, discipline is the glue that holds everything together and it starts at the top. If you expect discipline from your followers then you must be disciplined yourself, in your work, in your personal life, in the environment you create.

It's been over two decades since I first set out as a young coach. My first job was as assistant coach at the University of Hawaii. From there I went on to be an assistant at Syracuse, before I became the head coach at Boston University. I then went to the New York Knicks as an assistant coach for two years, before becoming the head coach of Providence College. In my second year at Providence we came out of nowhere to go to the Final Four and I became the national coach of the year. That led to becoming the head coach of the Knicks for two years, then on to Kentucky.

Even though I had worked with a lot of players and coached top professional and college teams to great success, in retrospect, it wasn't until I got to Kentucky in the spring of 1989 that I truly became a leader. Until then, I was just a basketball coach. Until then, I really hadn't thought a lot about the traits of leadership. I had spent those years consumed with learning my trade, building my career, trying to win games, and trying to move up the coaching ladder. I really didn't think of it in terms of leadership, even though so many of the traits that go into being a successful coach are leadership traits.

A coach is a teacher of fundamentals. A coach is a motivator. A coach is someone who looks after his players off the court. But there are many more facets to being a true leader; my experience at Kentucky taught me that.

When I first got to Kentucky in 1989 I was inheriting a storied program that had been wracked by scandal. It was similar to taking over the IBM of college basketball and finding the business at its absolute nadir. Kentucky was on NCAA probation because of recruiting violations, had been on the cover of *Sports Illustrated* with a headline that screamed out "Shame," and was, indeed, wallowing in its shame. It needed more than just a new basketball coach. It needed more than just wins and cheers and good players. It needed more than just time to heal its wounds.

It needed a leader.

Kentucky needed someone not only to bring back the glory days on the court, but also resurrect the image of this storied program. It needed someone to help give both the university and the state it represented its pride back. So when I came in, I had to do more than coach. I had to build up the program. I had to police it. I had to make it grow. I had to bring integrity back to Kentucky basketball. Most of all, I had to go from being a basketball coach to being a leader.

* * *

From those days in Kentucky to my current experience as head coach and president of the Boston Celtics, my search for the effective traits of leadership has been an ongoing one. It's a search that has taken me in many different directions, from reading about the great leaders in history to trial and error in my own professional life, to educating myself about successful leaders in all aspects of society. This book is the story of that search.

In a sense it is a journey, both philosophical and pragmatic, a journey that has gone on now for over two decades, from the small gym at Boston University to giving speeches to some of the leading companies in the country. I hope this book will expedite the process of learning about leadership for you.

Philosophically, we will explore the great leaders, both past and present. We will examine the traits that made them great, and the flaws that often were their Achilles' heels. Some things don't change and are as timeless as the concept of leadership itself. All leaders—from great historical figures to great classroom teachers—share certain traits that make people want to listen to them and follow them. We also will take a journey through contemporary leaders today, as we look to find the key reasons why they are so successful at leading others, be it people or companies.

Pragmatically, we will show you how to be a leader in today's changing world: the traits you need, the awareness you need, the knowledge you need to be a more effective leader. You will discover the traits and concepts that will work for you regardless of the arena in which you play. Learning these lessons of leadership has helped my career, my work, and, most important, my relationships with people. I know they can do the same for you.

LEAD
TO
SUCCEED

10 Traits
of Great
Leadership
in Business
and Life

1

HAVE A CONCRETE VISION

Back in the late seventies and early eighties at Boston University, even though I was a very young coach, I fundamentally understood the importance of a great work ethic. At the base of my coaching was always the belief that in order to do great things you must deserve them, and that you did that by being willing to put in the proper effort it takes to be successful at anything. It's the cornerstone of my philosophy, this sense that you must deserve victory.

I also understood the importance of team harmony and chemistry. I had been on teams all my life and had come to learn that teams that got along and helped one another—teams that had a common goal—had better chances to be successful than teams in which it seemed as if all the players were stars floating around in their own solar systems.

But as a young coach, I didn't understand the importance of having a vision, and I didn't understand the importance of being able to impart that vision to others. Eventually, I realized the people you are leading will have frustrations and failures, times when what they're doing is simply not working. When this happens (and rest assured it happens to everybody eventually), it's human nature for them to want to quit, either that or start to question what they're doing. Or else they look for people around them to blame, the inevitable finger-pointing that's so endemic in situations that are not successful.

What can stop people going through a tough time from taking these destructive, and self-destructive, actions?

Their vision.

All the great leaders have been people of great vision, men and women able to provide insight into what is possible. Vision is your view of the group's future, the place you want to be after the transformation is complete. For the people you're leading, vision is their belief in the overall game plan, their belief that this plan is in their best interest. Without this, all your dreams, all your ideas, can easily be derailed.

Ever since I was at Boston University, I've always been very conscious of creating a grand vision wherever I've coached. You simply cannot show up as the new leader and just wish everyone good luck. You must come in with a plan, a dramatic statement.

I remember the first meeting I had with the booster club when I got the Providence job. It was in the spring of 1985 at the Providence Civic Center, in a large upstairs banquet room that overlooked the court. Providence had been one of the bottom teams in the Big East since the conference had started six years before. There were limited talent, facilities, and resources. There also seemed to be a pall of negativity that hovered over everybody, this sense that they were never going to be successful in the Big East, and that had become one of life's sure things, right there with death and taxes. Everyone seemed to believe it. The players. The boosters. The fans. The media. It almost seemed as if there was "losing" water everyone had been drinking.

Still, my job was to get the people in that room to believe in a better future. During that meeting I tried not only to get them excited about the new era starting, but also to get them to contribute more money to the program and be more emotionally committed to it. In my mind, I was the new CEO of Providence College basketball and I had to get everyone to believe in the future.

The next day, a local sports writer compared me to a tent evangelist. He was right: That was my intention, to have the people in that room feed off my energy, my excitement, the tremendous passion I had for this new job and its potential. I wanted them to not only see my vision, but feel it, too. I wanted them to walk out of that room believing in possibilities.

"And when you go to bed at night," I finally said at the end of my speech, the energy in my voice, "I don't want you to count sheep. And I don't want you to worry about how much you owe on your Visa card. I don't want you to worry about your bills. I don't want you to worry about your troubles. I don't want you to think about your problems. When you go to bed at night"—my voice rising now, almost shouting, I looked out over the court and said, "when you go to bed at night I want you to dream about cutting down the nets."

Overdone? Probably.

Overstated? Maybe.

But that was my vision and I wanted everyone to know it. Just as Phil Knight had a vision of the future, back when he was driving up and down the West Coast to track meets, selling sneakers called Nikes out of his trunk, long before the clever television ads and the incredible success of his corporation. Just as all those people in those little computer shops talking a language nobody understood except them had a vision. Just as anyone who has a dream of one day building something greater has a vision.

What no one knew that day in the Providence Civic Center —even me—was that in less than two years we would cut down the nets in Louisville's Freedom Hall after having just qualified to go to the Final Four.

BE DIRECT

The message of a leader's first meeting with any organization is that the leader's vision is going to be their new reality, and the people in the organization are going to have to want to be a part of it. It's not a "yes" or "no" vote. It's not a democracy. In fact, they don't really have a choice at all. The bus is about to leave the station and they better be on it. But they are being invited to be part of the ride, and that's important.

In this first meeting you must not only seize the moment; you also have to take control. Right from the start. Like a general must take control of his troops, a leader must lead. Not in some undetermined future. Not in some fuzzy, unfocused way, but instantly, and in clear language that has a sense of urgency about it. Because if people do not believe that you believe in your vision there will be increased anxiety, doubt, cynicism, bad morale—all the things that poison a group and ultimately destroy it.

There always are going to be people who say, "I don't like this," or "I don't understand this," or "Why can't we do things the old way?"

They cannot be tolerated.

And in this first meeting you are conveying this, even if you are not being heavy-handed about it. Your message is: This is a new era and it starts right now and you really don't have a choice.

In the book *Leading Change*, John P. Kotter say the biggest mistake people make when trying to change organizations is to plunge ahead without establishing a high-enough sense of urgency in fellow managers and employees.

"This error is fatal," Kotter writes, "because transformations always fail to achieve their objectives when complacency levels are high."

He's right on target.

Your message has to be that change is not simply coming, it's already here. With a vengeance. Without that emphatic message it's too easy for people to rationalize; to say things like, "Things aren't that bad," or "We're simply in a little down cycle and that's just the way it goes," "Yes, we have some problems as a group, but I'm doing all right and that's the bottom line."

All of these are potential killers, instant impediments to what you're trying to do. People must leave that first meeting with a sense of urgency. Which is why I love the following Lou Holtz quote. When asked how long it was going to take him to transform the University of South Carolina football program, which was woeful when he took it over, he said, "Someone said, 'Rome wasn't built in a day.' I like to think that's because I wasn't born yet."

And even though Holtz did not win a game in his first season at South Carolina, he has the people of South Carolina fired up about its football program. He has the people around him believing in him and in his vision.

GET PEOPLE EXCITED

The other thing I try to do in this first meeting is stir passion.

Present the vision.

Then get people excited about it.

If you look at some of the people who are viewed as great leaders—John F. Kennedy and Martin Luther King Jr. as two prime examples—the one common denominator is passion. Both were able to move people emotionally and get them excited about the possibility of a better future. Want to see a textbook example of how a leader can stir passion? Listen to King's "I Have a Dream" speech. It is a classic in presenting a vision of the future and then stirring people's passion for that vision.

Why were African Americans so moved by King's speech in the sixties, even though they'd been subjected to so much racism and discrimination through the years? Even though King's speech sounded so pie-in-the-sky?

Because people want to believe. They want to see themselves in a better future. And even if you don't have the oratorical ability of Martin Luther King Jr., we can still learn from his method. The by-product of articulating your vision is that it starts to get people excited. You are talking about a better future for everyone and that raises possibilities. People don't want to fail. They don't want to wallow in mediocrity. They don't want to see their work as some endless journey that never really goes anywhere. They don't want to be unfulfilled. They don't want to be continually frustrated. People want to be successful. They want a better future. They want to see their dreams become actualized, they're just not sure how to go about it.

Your first job is to tell them this *can* happen.

Your second job is to tell them how.

Stirring passion is crucial, for the simple reason that leaders without passion have problems. What's the point of having a vision for a turnaround of your company if you're not able to articulate it? What's the point of having a vision of the future if you cannot get people excited about it?

Raising people's passions chips away at the doubt. This is vital because you want people to begin to feel the future can be better for them. Yes, they're entering a time of change, but they don't have to fear that things are going to be worse. Instead, you want them believing that this is a new beginning for everyone, full of hope and promise. You have to show them the future.

The next step is to tell them how this is going to happen. Change raises most people's anxiety level. So you must try to assuage the fear and quell the doubt. You do this by telling the people the methods you're going to use. The vision and the methods used to reach that vision must be similar.

In every first meeting I've had with a team, I tell the players the story of the full-court press, one of the staples of my defensive philosophy as a basketball coach. I tell them how it caused twenty-three turnovers a game in 1987, the year my Providence College team went to the Final Four. I tell them that without the press we were a very mediocre team that year, that the press was our weapon, our edge. It was the reason we were able to beat more talented teams. I show them what the press accomplished, so that they can see the whole, what the fruits of their labor will one day accomplish. That's the process: Show them the whole, then start implementing the parts.

This is vital.

You must tell people what their hard work is one day going to get them. You just can't institute a work ethic, essentially tell people they're going to work harder than they've ever had in the past, tell them that there is going to be change and they are going to have to adapt to it whether they want to or not, and not tell them there will be a reward. This is not the Age of the Pharaohs, where people are going to push rocks day after day in the noon-time sun just because the king tells them to. People are not going to give you blind obedience. They are not going to do what you want them to do just because you say they're going to. They are not going to blindly follow you simply because you're their new leader.

You have to tell them what's in it for them. We all want to know that if we work hard and give our allegiance to the group that we're going to be rewarded for it. No one wants to think that his hard work, all his energy, is simply going to benefit someone else. It's essential, then, that you convey this message in your first meeting, so there's no chance for misunderstanding. This will help combat the inevitable doubt and anxiety that's inherent in any kind of change.

In a company it's the same script.

It's essential that the people directly under you on the organizational ladder both understand and share your vision, for they will be the ambassadors of your vision to the people who work underneath them. They're the ones on the front line, the ones who will have much more interaction with the employees. Therefore, they must not only share and understand your vision, but also be able to articulate it.

In July of 1999, I read a newspaper article that showed a good example of communicating vision. Chris Palmer, the coach of the Cleveland Browns, the new expansion team in the National Football League, said two weeks before the team's first training camp that he was going to screen for his players some old films of the Browns' glory days: Jim Brown breaking tackles, Bernie Kosar throwing touchdown passes.

"I want the players to know what it means to play for the Cleveland Browns," he said. "What it means to play in this city and in front of these fans."

That's an example of showing the vision.

Communicating tradition is a good way to present your vision for your organization. Every five or six years, a new generation will lose sight of the group's tradition unless it's constantly reinforced. Tradition is not something we can take for granted. It must constantly be reinforced or one day you will wake up and it will be gone. Especially now, in an age when leaders move from job to job with more frequency, remaining aware of and continuing tradition is an important message for new leaders to convey.

JUMP IN THE BOAT WITH THEM

In the beginning—when you are new in your role as a leader—you also have to gain the respect of the people you are leading.

How do you do that? Why should someone follow you, when you haven't proved anything yet? Why should people give you their allegiance?

From day one, you must convince them you're all in the boat together. And you can't just verbalize this. You have to get into the boat with them. Your message is: "We're in the boat together and we're going to succeed or fail together."

Understandably, this isn't going to happen overnight. By its very nature respect must develop over time, based on both results and trust. It's imperative, though, that you expedite the process, do everything in your power from the beginning to let people know your fate is aligned with their fate, that you cannot succeed unless they succeed, that this is a partnership.

An important way to begin this process is to show your employees you're concerned about them.

One of the first things I did when I came to the Celtics in 1997 was to begin pushing for a new practice facility. Part of my motivation, certainly, was that the Celtics had made themselves noncompetitive when it came to facilities. They were using part of the gym at Brandeis College in suburban Boston, and while it always was a good relationship with the school, the locker room was cramped, the weight room was insufficient, the facilities were simply not good enough for an NBA team on the eve of the millennium.

I was convinced we needed new facilities to be able to attract free agents, something all NBA teams must be able to do. Professional athletes are just like other valued performers in today's business climate. They want to be courted. They want to be recruited. They want to feel important. They want to go work for companies that have great facilities and in a buyer's market that's what they're going to do. I had done a similar thing at Kentucky, redoing the offices, putting in a first-class weight room. When you're trying to recruit quality players to your organization, these things are essential.

Besides, inferior facilities send a negative signal to your players. The inherent message is that the organization is something less than first class. This is one of the worst possible messages you can give your employees. Upgrading facilities is a tangible way to tell employees that things are indeed changing, that it's not merely hollow words and empty promises. It also shows them that you want them to have the best work environment possible.

This is probably even more important in today's corporate culture, when the technology is changing rapidly. Few things send a deadlier message to your employees than working with what they perceive to be outdated equipment. It's an instant morale killer. You must keep pace with your competition, and the inability to keep pace with the best equipment sends the message that you cannot keep pace with your competition.

Your underlying message—one that must be constantly reinforced—is that you *care* about the people you are leading. You value them. You care about them as individuals. You care about their work environment. You care about their success.

This cannot be stressed enough.

All employees want to feel they they're important. It's up to you to see that that happens. Obviously, one way is by salary. But it's not the only way. Praise. Encouragement. Recognition. Some form of personal touch: These are ways to not only reward people, but to make them feel important.

Because your vision can't be an "I-my" vision. It is not just about how I, Rick Pitino, will turn around a team and get all the credit. It must be a collective vision. It also must be a blueprint based around hope and morale, the sense that we're all in this together; that everyone has a vested stake in turning the company around; that everyone will benefit, not just the leader. You don't want people to mentally dangle, to exist in some gray netherworld of doubt, afraid of the future, uncertain about their fate. There's always going to be uncertainty in any new leadership situation, a certain built-in stress, that's a given. People always have a fear of the unknown, an instinctive reluctance to change. You must not only understand this, but deal with it.

* * *

Look at what usually happens with a failing company.

The first event is the CEO is let go. Then a new one comes in and the first thing he does is lay off 20 percent of the workforce. The result is a climate of negativity and doubt. The employees start to wonder who is next. Everyone worries about their own fate. The atmosphere is already poisoned.

Instead, let's look at a different scenario:

The new leader comes in and right away he starts talking about a new vision for the company. Not "my" vision. Not an individual vision, but a collective vision. This is fundamental. The first thing you must do when you assume a leadership role is to build morale. You already know that morale is poor, the climate is full of negativity and doubt. This always happens with change, for people don't like change. It destroys their comfort level and makes them fear the future.

Every time I've entered a new college coaching situation I know the players I'm inheriting have a lot of anxiety. It's human nature. Both change, and the prospect of change, raise anxiety. Most people are infinitely more comfortable with the familiar, the known. Change is disorienting, upsetting. The remaining players, therefore, are saying to themselves that since I didn't recruit them I will have no allegiance to them and discard them as quickly as I can. They are understandably nervous and unsure. Who wouldn't be?

So the first thing I try to do is lessen everyone's anxiety and calm everyone down. I tell the remaining players that they are automatically "my players," for the simple reason that I believe in quick turnarounds, and in order to do that I need them, not my own recruits in the future.

That first meeting is critical. You don't get a second chance to make a first impression and the team's first impression of me is going to stay in their minds for a long time after the first meeting.

More important, it's the place where I must articulate my vision of the future and show them how we all can reach that future together. I must show them they can be successful, that it's not simply some pipe dream, some flight of fancy that's unrealistic. I want them to know that from now on there's a purpose to everything, that this is a new beginning and they all are a part of it. That from now on we are going to share everything together, day by day.

I want people to leave that first meeting feeling encouraged. Sure, some people will be cynical. Sure, some people will have doubts. That's human nature, too. I have no doubt that those Providence College players had doubts when I became their coach in the spring of 1985 and told them of my vision of the future. Sure, they wondered about me.

But they also had been given a glimpse of a better future.

Your goal, as a leader, is to eventually get everyone to share your vision.

Obviously, achieving this goal is easier the more success you have as a group. One of the commonalities of professional athletic teams that do well is how much easier it is for these teams to get their players to work hard in the off-season. I read an article in which Mike Shanahan, the coach of the Denver Broncos, said that the number of players committed to their off-season conditioning program rose dramatically after the Broncos won their first Super Bowl. That made sense to me. Those players had reached the mountain top and enjoyed the fruits of their success and were willing to do the work to stay there.

It is in the beginning, when there is little or no success yet, that this is infinitely more difficult. Doubt and second-guessing are always going to be part of the landscape then. There are always going to be people who don't believe in you, the ones that have to be convinced. There are always going to be some people waiting for you to fail, in the hope that they can go back to doing things the old way.

Obviously, the more success you have, the more people will give you the benefit of the doubt. For example, when Bill Parcells became the coach of the Jets, the players he was inheriting were more likely to initially buy into his vision because they were well aware of Parcells's great reputation as a football coach. Even so, there are always going to be doubters, those who want to go back to the old way, the familiar way. There are always going to be people who question you.

When I became the coach of the Celtics I knew that there were probably a few players I was inheriting who didn't want to work as hard as I expected them to. I'm sure that there were a few who considered me a college coach, even though I had coached the Knicks for two years in the mid-eighties. It's naive to think that everyone is initially going to unconditionally accept your vision.

Still, you must be sure that everyone is aware of your vision of the future and working at those methods to one day reach it. It is a clear vision that will get people through the difficult times.

It's vision that will allow them to survive periods of doubt and frustration. It's vision that will allow them to survive adversity. It's vision that allows your organization to always be moving forward rather than stagnating in negativity and regret, and it's vision that's the summit for which you're always reaching.

KEY CHAPTER POINTS

- **Be Direct** People must understand what your vision is and that they are being asked to be a part of it, but that it's really not a democracy. Change is coming, and they are either going to have to buy into it or get left behind.

- **Get People Excited** There is no underestimating passion. People have to not only know what's in it for them, but be made to feel positive about the coming change.

- **Jump in the Boat with Them** People must know that everyone is in it together: They must understand that your success as a leader is linked to their success.

STEVE JOBS

At first glance, Steve Jobs would seem to be an unlikely candidate to become one of the most successful and influential men of the past twenty-five years. There's nothing in his background that would indicate he was destined for success, much less greatness. He was a college dropout, a loner who studied philosophy and immersed himself in the counterculture lifestyle. Jobs was not unlike thousands of other young people living in California at the time.

But lurking beneath that surface was a young man with true vision. Jobs dreamed of creating a user-friendly personal computer that would be available to and affordable for everyone. At that time, computers were big and burdensome. Most were owned by large companies and a few computer "geeks." Jobs wanted to change all that and he did.

While working as a video game designer at Atari, Inc., Jobs, then twenty-one, and his friend Steve Wozniak, twenty-six, managed to scrape together $13,000 by selling virtually all their possessions. It wasn't much money, but with that capital base and credit begged from local electronics suppliers they were able to start their new company. In 1976, Jobs and Wozniak put together their first computer, which they called the Apple I. They designed it in Jobs's bedroom and built the prototype in his garage. It was marketed at the price of $666.

The following year, Jobs and Wozniak improved upon their initial invention by building the Apple II. In 1984, they introduced the Macintosh. It was this computer, probably more than any other, that set the standard for what was to come. It also put a sizable dent in the IBM mystique.

The Apple II made Jobs and Wozniak very rich men. The Apple II had earnings of $139 million during its first three years on the market. Within the first six years of its formation, Apple was selling more than 650,000 personal computers a year. Eventually, it grew into a two-billion-dollar company. It's not surprising that in 1989, *Inc.* magazine named Jobs the Entrepreneur of the Decade.

But building a successful company and running it are two entirely different propositions. While Jobs and Wozniak were certainly entrepreneurs with a high-minded vision and a clear idea of what they believed they could achieve, neither had any formal business or leadership training. So how were they able to turn a two-man dream that began in a garage into one of the richest and most profitable companies in the world? By going against the grain, that's how.

From day one, Jobs and Wozniak kept their vision intact and they communicated it at every turn. Even more important, they hired people who understood the vision. And when times were tough, as they were in those early days, Jobs and Wozniak never lost sight of the goals they were trying to accomplish.

Jobs and Wozniak were also brilliant strategists when it came to hiring employees. Their approach was radical and unorthodox: They would survey the situation, decide what was needed, then go out and hire the most experienced person in that area. They needed a marketing edge, so they hired one of the best marketers in the business, Regis McKenna. When they needed an experienced person to become Apple's president, they lured John Sculley away from PepsiCo.

It was a very nonhierarchical way of hiring people. It was also the complete opposite to the approach taken by most entrepreneurs, who tend to be possessive and overly authoritative. Jobs and Wozniak were willing to share their power. They motivated people by including them and treating them with great respect and dignity.

Jobs has continued his successful and innovative ways. He is currently chairman and CEO of Pixar, a computer animation studio he cofounded in 1986. The company's first feature film, *Toy Story*, was released by Disney in November 1995 and became the third-highest-grossing animated film of all time. *Toy Story 2*, released in the fall of 1999, won a Golden Globe and became the biggest success of the holiday season.

Steve Jobs is proof that there is no single cookie-cutter image when it comes to leaders. He went against the grain in many ways, even to the point of breaking some of the most sacred rules of leadership. But what was important, and what enabled him to succeed, was that he always stayed true to himself and to the goals he sought to accomplish.

2

BE YOUR OWN MESSENGER

Many times new leaders will have an excellent vision and are also initially able to sell that vision: their team or organization is excited, or at least willing to give it a try. The vision is out there like some high-flying flag. The methods to reach that vision have been instituted. All the pieces seem to be in place.

Then, after a seemingly perfect setup, everything simply stalls out.

Why?

Because there's been very little follow-up. After they've had their initial kickoff meeting with the team, leaders often make the assumption that people now know what to do 100 percent, and now it's up to them to go ahead and do it, no problem.

It's an incorrect assumption.

Leaders must constantly reinforce the goals of the group, all the time.

This is something I'm always doing. Every day I talk to my team about what we're trying to accomplish. Some days it might only be a few minutes, but it's always there. They hear about what we're trying to accomplish every day in some manner, shape, or form, so that there's no uncertainty about what our goals are. No wavering, no doubt. Nothing is left to chance. The goals always are positively reinforced.

Leaders must be "hands-on." If they're not, things start to slide.

You can see that by how most players reacted during the NBA "lockout" that lasted from June of 1998 until January of 1999. You would assume that most players would have come back in great shape because basketball is their livelihood and they all know that being in great shape is the cornerstone to being successful as a professional athlete. That wasn't the reality. On our entire Celtics team we only had two players who reported to training camp in great shape—Dana Barros and Ron Mercer. Without the goals of the group constantly being reinforced, most of the players had let them slide.

That's why I talk to my team every day; this reaffirms our vision, constantly keeps it out there. You can't do it enough.

Regardless of how good your message is, people are not going to assimilate it the first time they hear it.

Think of it this way: Your message to someone is fighting innumerable things that person is hearing that day. We live in an age of sensory overload, a constant bombardment of images and information that we all assimilate every day, everything from television and radio commercials to the Internet, to things people say around the water cooler at work. Your message is only one of them. The key, therefore, is to keep saying it over and over, until it becomes a mantra people keep hearing in their heads. This is what the advertising business figured out a long time ago: It's not just the message, it's the message heard over and over again.

You can't assume that people are going to understand your message simply because they've heard it often. Not today. Trying to capture the hearts and minds of your employees is an ongoing process, virtually a daily process. There are always going to be a percentage of people who never really heard your vision in the first place or who have only given lip service to it. Rest assured they're not going to remember it unless you virtually hit them over the head with it.

There also are people on the fence, waiting to see how things play out. Then there are the others who only faintly understood your message in the beginning and who no doubt forgot the gist of it soon after that first meeting. You can't let these people simply exist in a vacuum. If they do, they quickly will revert back to their old habits and their old way of viewing things.

Your message must constantly be out there. The more direct and simple you make it the better off it will be.

Your message can't be fuzzy and vague. You can't give people any possible reason to misunderstand. And your message can't be layered with jargon. One of the biggest turnoffs to people is to talk in jargon and psychobabble. All this does is get in the way, causing confusion. You want to be as clear and concise as possible in all your meetings, direct and to the point. You are not trying to impress people with big words and lofty phrases. Your goal is not to have them walk out of meetings saying how smart you are. Your goal is to have them walking out of meetings understanding what you are saying.

One of the mistakes I made my first year with the Celtics was that my meetings were too long. Meetings that drag on are counterproductive. People's attention wanders. They get distracted and start to tune out the speaker. Ultimately, they end up praying for the meeting to end more than they listen to what's going on. So your rule is simple: Get in, get out.

DON'T LET OTHERS DO YOUR JOB

One of the biggest turnoffs I get is when someone's secretary calls me and says, "Hold for Mr. So-and-So."

My first instinct is that the person calling believes their time is more important than my time, that I have nothing to do but hold for this person. My second instinct is this person is "big-timing" me. Either way, it sends the wrong message. It shows a lack of respect for the person you're dealing with, even if that's not your intention.

The message you want to give is that the person you're dealing with is important and the best way to do this is to deliver the message yourself. Pick up the phone yourself. Write the note yourself. Write the memo yourself. Deal with it yourself, especially if you want this message to be accurate.

Going through a third party only complicates things. So many times messages get misinterpreted, or else they are delivered out of context or with a different tone. Regardless, the message the person receives is somehow different from the one you sent. I see this all the time with Tim Sypher, who works for me. I often use him to deliver messages to people and invariably the message gets distorted.

Why?

Not because Sypher relays it wrong. It's because his style is short and to the point. His tone is invariably different than my tone would be, thus the context is never the same. On the other hand, Rick Avare, my business manager, is so overprotective of me that any message given to him to give to someone else becomes so sugar-coated it all but melts in their mouths. Two different people. Two different styles. Same result. My message rarely gets delivered quite the way I want it to be delivered.

With messages that are relatively unimportant this is obviously not a big deal. With important messages, though, it's a very big deal. With important messages you have to be the messenger, you have to be the one that assures that that particular message is delivered the way you want it delivered.

For example:

Let's say I have to cut a player. This is one of the hardest things to do in coaching, especially when that player has worked hard and done everything you asked him to do. Now you have to let him go and the easiest thing for me would be to abdicate and let Chris Wallace, my general manager, do it. I don't do that, for in my mind that's like the doctor having the nurse tell the patient he has a serious illness. Whenever possible, I try to tell that player myself that I am letting him go.

Sometimes the timing of that makes that impossible, because this is usually the scenario: First you do the deal, then you tell the players. What can sometimes happen, though, is word of the deal gets out before the players can be notified. That's what happened when I traded Popeye Jones to Denver in the summer of 1999, as part of the deal that sent Ron Mercer to the Nuggets for Danny Fortson. I tried to reach him and left a message for him on his voice mail, but by the time he got it he already had heard of the trade from someone else. I felt bad that I didn't get a chance to tell him personally, because Popeye is one of the finest gentlemen in the game.

Every time I haven't told someone one-on-one it's come back to haunt me. That's what leaders do: deliver the difficult message personally.

Communicating directly is important not just with the big things, but also with day-to-day issues.

For example:

Let's say one of your employees is deficient in a certain area. The easiest thing to do is tell one of your assistants to relay that message to that employee. Often this is the way things are done, working downward through the chain of command. Rest assured, though, it means more to that person if the message comes from you.

That doesn't mean I don't utilize my staff, because sometimes the message would be better served coming from them.

For example:

Suppose I hear rumors of alcohol abuse about one of my players. Confronting that person myself might be the wrong approach; he would likely be more intimidated by me and might be less likely to offer up the truth if he were scared. Instead, I use one of my assistants to mention to the particular player—almost in an off-hand manner—that that rumor is out there, essentially to gauge that player's reaction. This approach—the use of one of your assistants as a buffer—is not confrontational and is probably better suited when you are simply looking for more information.

It's important to understand that people often hear what they want to hear. In this context things often get misinterpreted, especially criticism, and especially criticism of young people. Pete Carril, the legendary former basketball coach at Princeton, probably said it best when he said, "What we used to think of as coaching they think is criticism." You criticize someone today and invariably they view it as an attack.

In this environment, then, it's imperative that you decide the tone. You decide the context in which the criticism is given. You can't afford your message to be misinterpreted. It's tough enough to criticize someone, never mind having it be misinterpreted.

To avoid this, you must be your own messenger. How did I learn this? Easy. From sending out so many bad messages. From letting other people deliver them for me and from not understanding that sometimes the tone in which a message is delivered can be as important as the message itself.

Leading a group of people—each with his or her own attitude and history and personality—is difficult enough without your message being taken the wrong way.

* * *

When I first got to Kentucky in the spring of 1989, quickly becoming aware of the magnitude of the problems that were hovering over the Kentucky basketball program, one of the things I realized was that there were several NCAA rules that were being broken. One obvious one was that the players routinely were given freebies around Lexington. It was just the way it was, and odds are that many of the people handing out the freebies probably didn't even realize they were breaking NCAA rules, but they were.

So I set out to stop it. Not only did I tell the players that the way things had been done in the past were over, I went from restaurant to restaurant, from bar to bar, telling the owners not to give any more freebies to Kentucky basketball players.

At one sporting goods store that was giving discounts to players I told the owner he had to stop it.

"You're not going to tell me what to do," the owner said. "I give discounts to many people."

"If you don't stop this," I told him, "I'm going to call the *Lexington Herald-Leader* and tell them to let the public know that you are the reason why Kentucky basketball is going to get the 'death penalty' from the NCAA."

Understandably, the sporting goods owner changed his mind.

Another time, two of our Kentucky players—Jeff Sheppard and Jared Prickett—had lunch at a Lexington restaurant with a local banker.

"Did you guys pay for your lunch?" I asked them after I found out about the lunch.

"No," they said. "But it was only hamburgers. Probably only cost him about ten dollars."

"Then go back and pay him ten dollars."

Then I called The Guy and asked him who he was. When he told me, I asked him, "Why does a twenty-eight-year-old banker want to have lunch with two nineteen-year-olds?"

It simply didn't pass the "smell test" with me. I then called the guy's boss to try to find out more about him, because one of the things I first tried to do at Kentucky was stop the influence of the boosters, one of the things that had led to much of the trouble with the Kentucky basketball program in the first place.

The point is that I didn't wait for the "booster problem" to go away by itself. Nor did I simply tell my players they weren't to socialize with boosters anymore. Nor did I just have someone on my staff spread my message. I was my own messenger and stopped a potential problem.

* * *

There are times when you feel you are doing a hundred different things at once. Certainly, there are times when you simply have too much on your plate to get to everything yourself. I often get as many as fifty pieces of correspondence a day so I simply cannot answer every one myself or that's all I would be doing. I must delegate. The ones that can be handled by my secretary are done that way. Yet I must be aware of what is being said and the message that is going forth.

In the book *1001 Ways to Reward Employees*, Bob Nelson writes that numerous motivational studies show that employees typically place a high value on getting information about their job, their performance, and how their company is doing. When that communication is written it is even more effective.

There are other ways to communicate, too.

One of the ways to do this is get out of the office and circulate. The leader who always is in his office behind a big desk, perceived as unapproachable, eventually will pay for that management style. You can't be aloof. You can't be perceived as autocratic, someone far removed from everyone else. Again, one of your initial mission statements was that you and the people you are leading are "in the boat together," your respective futures linked together. Being perceived as unapproachable flies in the face of that.

COMMUNICATE WHAT YOU WANT

So much of good leadership rests on your ability to get your message across. The ability to communicate effectively is one of your best weapons. From establishing your vision at the very first meeting to constantly reinforcing that vision at every opportunity, good communication is key. What's the point of having a vision if you can't share it with the people you lead?

One of the things I've learned through the years is you can't underestimate the ability to communicate well. I once thought that I always had been a good communicator, but in retrospect, there was a time I really wasn't. When I was younger I made the mistake so many people make: I was trying to win conversations with people, not necessarily relate to them. Too often, I saw conversations as contests, with winners and losers. I wanted to win arguments. I wanted people to see my side and agree with me. I was too concerned with being right.

Gradually, though, I began to realize that the more I listened to people the better I seemed to communicate with them.

One way I learned this was by going into so many homes during recruiting visits. In the beginning, as a young coach, I did all the traditional things to sell my school: I talked about our basketball program. I talked about the school's academic opportunities. I talked about our campus. I talked about our facilities. I talked about our schedule. I talked about the opportunities that would be there after graduation. I talked about virtually anything I could think of that might lure that recruit to sign with my school.

And invariably, this would be the scenario: After the visit I would go back to the car and one of my assistant coaches would say, "You were great, Coach. You covered everything. I really think we're going to get the kid."

Then we wouldn't get that particular recruit and we would all wonder why.

Gradually, though, I changed my approach.

I would go into a recruit's home and say very little. Instead, I would listen, both to the kid and his parents. And invariably, afterward in the car, my assistant coach would shake his head and say, "I don't know, Coach. You forgot to mention the new weight room and you didn't talk about the Christmas trip and you really didn't talk about the schedule enough. I don't feel good about this one."

You guessed it. Often, we would get that kid, and the feedback would be that the recruit and his parents felt comfortable with me.

Why?

Because I had listened more and started building a trust.

It wasn't so much what I said, or didn't day, as my *approach*.

The art of communication is about relating to people and you do that best by listening to them. There are other things to pay attention to: looking at people when they speak, concentrating on what people are saying instead of thinking about what you're going to say next, trying to understand where people are coming from, what their concerns are. These things make people feel comfortable; make them feel that you're talking to them, not just talking *at* them. Talking to a group is about providing enthusiasm and passion, about trying to use your skills to move the group in a certain direction. It is about energy.

Speaking to one person is about listening.

* * *

As a leader, what you're trying to do is build bridges.

Let me give you two examples:

One of the biggest disappointments of my coaching life was Rodrick Rhodes. He had been a great high school player at St. Anthony's in Jersey City, New Jersey, and was one of the top recruits in the country. When we recruited him to Kentucky it was a significant coup. But it never really happened for Rodrick at Kentucky. Certainly not in the way he envisioned.

In retrospect, he didn't have great shot selection. The knock on him always had been that he wasn't a great perimeter shooter. So it often seemed as though he was always trying to prove he could hit the perimeter jump shot, when in reality he was a "slasher," someone very good at taking the ball to the hoop. I always had the sense Rodrick was listening to other people tell him he had to show the NBA scouts that he could make the perimeter shot. Ultimately, it was to the detriment of his game.

Eventually, he decided to leave Kentucky after his junior year, transferring to the University of Southern California.

I could have been the perfect scapegoat for Rodrick. He could have blamed all his frustrations on me, his coach. He did not. What did he do? He went the other way. He publicly said I had treated him fairly, that I had been honest with him. In doing so, he built a bridge with me for life.

There's a postscript to this story.

A couple of years ago I got a call from the Houston Rockets. They were thinking of drafting Rodrick, who was then a senior at USC, and wanted my opinion of Rodrick. I was with two friends from Kentucky at the time and they couldn't believe I was praising Rodrick, a guy who really hadn't worked out at Kentucky, so ardently to the Rockets, telling them what a quality person Rodrick was, how he would work hard for their team.

Why did I react that way, they wanted to know?

"Because Rodrick built a bridge with me," I said. "And when you build bridges you can keep crossing them."

The second example is Dee Brown, who was on the Celtics when I took over.

Dee and I were never close when he played for me on the Celtics. Dee wanted to play more minutes and we had Ron Mercer at his position. I had problems with him in practice, as he was a veteran, and we had philosophical differences. So when I traded him he could have reacted negatively. A lot of players would have. Dee did not. Instead, he said, "This is a business," and that Rick Pitino had to do what he thought was best for the Boston Celtics.

In his public comments, Dee Brown was a professional. He, too, built a bridge.

Both Rodrick Rhodes and Dee Brown took the high road in these stories and displayed good personal leadership skills that can serve as an example to others, whether you're on a team or at a company.

That's what I'm always telling Antoine Walker, whom I've

known for a long time, even since recruiting him to go to Kentucky.

He was probably an underrecruited high school All-American, a great talent who needed to be channeled in the right direction. He was perceived as a selfish player. He was brash. He talked a lot of trash. He turned a lot of people off with his behavior.

Was this the truth?

Not really.

What he was at the time was sixteen years of age.

When he was a freshman, I was always disciplining him for one reason or another. He was always being sent to run on the treadmill. He was very difficult to coach.

But Antoine always took it. He always knew what I was doing. He always had respect and loyalty. And he always knew what was good for him.

Yet, now that he plays for me with the Celtics, it does not help that I was Antoine's college coach. We've been together five years now and that's a long time. It seems like I'm forever trying to get him to understand a certain philosophy. I want him to pass the ball more because he can dominate a game with his passing skills. I always tell him he should model himself after Magic Johnson, and that's the highest compliment I can give a player.

Sometimes, it seems like it's an ongoing struggle to wait for him to mature, but the NBA is not about conflicts and confrontations. Conflicts steamroll. They bring other people into the dispute. They complicate things. You don't want to choose sides, such as, for example, when you are in a disagreement with a person and you say to a third person, "Will you tell him he's wrong?"

That's a terrible strategy. You are asking someone to choose sides. You are escalating the disagreement.

My attitude with a player is this: This is the style we play. If you don't want to play it, we will try and move you.

Let's go back to Antoine. I won't harp on his failures, because it's difficult for young people to own up to them anyway. That's my biggest problem with him: He must learn to be smarter about owning up to his responsibilities and communicating responsibly. And I am trying to teach him how to do it, because you have to do it. This is a business and we all have to be shrewd about it.

In the summer of 1999, we were running a summer league in Boston and our team was comprised of mostly free agents. Yet Antoine publicly said he was going to play, even though he didn't have to. Then, in the end, he didn't show up and it became a story in the newspapers. Now, it was fine if he didn't want to play; I knew his ankle was still bothering him. But why say you're going to play, then not show up? He needed to explain why he wasn't going to play. That's the shrewd thing to do.

The point is that what we say is important. How we act is important. Nothing we do takes place in a vacuum because others judge us by how we follow through on our promises and how we conduct ourselves professionally. Remember, our goal is to build bridges, not to burn them.

KNOW THE DANGERS OF ASSUMPTIONS

You can't blame people for what they don't know.

Telling people they *should have known* what you meant, or that they *should have understood* what you wanted them to do is an instant recipe for failure. People should not be expected to be mind readers. Nor should they have to decipher what you want by having to go through a maze of verbal clues.

Many misunderstandings occur this way. You assume that people know what you're thinking and when their actions reveal otherwise, your first reaction is to blame them or else think less of them. You assume that somehow people are on the same wavelength as you, even if their actions invariably tell you they are not. If people are constantly misunderstanding your messages, odds are that you are not communicating them very well.

You also have to be careful not to promise too much to the people you lead. Overpromising is a trap into which it's very easy to fall.

Let's say someone comes in to see you. They want something—a raise, a promotion, a promise of something happening in the future. It's human nature to want to appease them, to make that person feel hopeful. So you give them the hope of a promise. Not a real promise etched in stone, but the hope of a promise, whether it's going to be a promotion, a raise, whatever. You sort of dangle it out there; you say something vague like, "I'll see what I can do."

But this is what happens:

That person leaves your office and you essentially forget about it. After all, you are having these kinds of conversations with people all the time. And you haven't actually promised them anything, so what's to remember?

But, believe me, that person remembers.

Although you didn't intend to, you have led that person on, given him or her the hope that that promotion is just around the corner if he or she keeps working hard.

Promising something raises a person's hopes. And when those hopes are not delivered that person is going to resent you. He is going to think you lied to him, betrayed him in some way.

Now you might be entirely innocent in all this. But you have gotten yourself into trouble by 1) either promising too much, or 2) promising what you can't deliver.

Parents do this all the time.

How many times have you heard a child say, "But you promised." Or else, they will say, "But you said . . ." Often you have no idea what they're talking about, having long since forgotten the conversation. But they remember. You can count on that.

So the rule is: Watch out what you promise and write down what you promise.

Here is a case in point:

When we drafted Chauncey Billups and Ron Mercer in our first draft with the Celtics, in June of 1997, I called them the "Celtic backcourt of the future." That was the mistake I made. Instead of simply saying we had drafted two good young players whom I hoped would be able to grow with us, I said too much. We had just taken Billups with the third pick in the draft, and Mercer with the sixth. They were two popular picks and I was caught up in the excitement of the evening.

It doesn't matter that I didn't know at the time that Billups was more of a "two" guard than a point guard. That's the problem with college "two" guards trying to convert to being a point guard. Nor did it matter that at the end of his second season in the NBA Mercer would want $8 to 10 million a year and we simply couldn't afford that. All that mattered was that we traded Billups to Toronto midway through his rookie year, traded Mercer to Denver in the summer after his second year, and that the "Celtic backcourt of the future," never materialized. I made a big mistake.

I overstated the situation in all my excitement.

The other common mistake is to act quickly on assumptions without knowing all the facts.

For example:

In November of 1999 the grandmother of Dana Barros—our backup point guard who grew up in Boston—died. At the wake I couldn't believe that there were no Celtic players there. Were they that insensitive? Were they that oblivious to a teammate's grief?

I assumed the worst.

My first instinct was to bring this up to the entire team, to make an issue out of it, but then I decided to seek more facts. I called Pervis Ellison, one of Dana's teammates, into my office, and in the course of our conversation, I said, "Pervis, you're one of the veterans on this team, so can you tell me why none of you players went to Dana's grandmother's wake?"

"We were going to," Pervis said, "and we all chipped in to

buy flowers, but Dana told us not to come, that he wanted to take care of it himself."

So if I hadn't spoken to Pervis and gotten more facts I would have overreacted.

The lesson?

Don't assume you know what's going on before you know all the facts. Often you will be wrong and you will embarrass yourself and others.

The other lesson? Try to deal with as many things one-on-one as you can. By dealing with Pervis Ellison, I was able to get facts that changed my initial assumption.

This is especially true when your team appears to be stagnant. Any group is a little like a stock price. It's either going up, down, or just treading water. And when your group is merely treading water you're naturally going to have many assumptions why this is happening. So you need information. You need facts. You need to know as much about the situation as you possibly can to get to a potential solution. And the more you do yourself in pursuit of this, the better off you're going to be.

KEY CHAPTER POINTS

- **Don't Let Others Do Your Job** The best messages are the ones that you deliver yourself.

- **Communicate What You Want** People cannot be blamed for what they don't know. It's your job to make sure that the people you are leading understand your message.

- **Know the Dangers of Assumptions** As soon as you start assuming things, you're headed for trouble. You can't simply assume that people know what you want or that they know all the facts you do. One-on-one meetings are often the best way to keep everyone informed and in the loop.

MOSES

Throughout recorded history, few leaders have been more cele-
brated and venerated than Moses. He is regarded as the greatest
of all the ancient Israeli prophets, the man who walked into the
palace of his captor and delivered his people from the chains of
bondage and slavery.

The mere mention of his name conjures an image of a man
filled with strength, courage, and fearlessness. To say the name
Moses is to say the word *freedom*.

Of course, he wasn't alone in his undertaking. Let's face it:
Moses had a pretty good boss.

Given that, the tendency might be to dismiss him as simply the instrument through which God worked His divine plan.
To do that is not only a mistake, it's also shortsighted. While it
is certainly true that God provided the miracles—the parting of
the Red Sea, the plagues, turning the Nile to blood, the Ten
Commandments—it remained for Moses to lead his people
during the forty years they wandered through the desert before
finally being allowed to enter the Promised Land. And it was
during this period that Moses' leadership skills were put to the
test.

As is often the case with great leaders, his followers were
unable, or perhaps unwilling, to appreciate the person who was
leading them. This was certainly true of the Israelites. They had
no idea how fortunate they were to have Moses on their side.
While they were grumbling and complaining about their desper-
ate plight, Moses was standing before God, appealing for their
lives.

Despite having the yoke of slavery lifted from their shoulders, the Israelites had corrupted themselves to such an extent that God threatened to consume them and start over with just Moses and his descendants. But Moses, always the leader, stood up and defended them against God's anger. By arguing brilliantly on their behalf, Moses was able to persuade God to forgive them and allow His plan to unfold.

Even later, when the people again angered God to such an extent that He wanted to strike them down, it was Moses who pleaded with Him to leave the Israelites unharmed. Moses was always there for his people. Although they failed him on numerous occasions, not once did he ever fail them.

It's easy to lose Moses the man behind Moses the miracle worker. However, the reality is that Moses' life ran the gamut of human experiences. It's obvious he had a forgiving heart and an understanding spirit. And his compassion for the weaknesses of his people seemed to have no limits. Even when his beloved sister Miriam spoke against him and was punished by God, Moses was quick to defend her.

Moses was also a truly humble man. When God first charged him with the task of leading the Israelites out of Egypt, Moses argued that he wasn't up to the challenge. He had to be convinced that he could do it. He even argued to such an extent that God became exasperated with him. But once Moses was convinced, once he shed the cloak of self-doubt that tormented him, he proved himself to be a leader with extraordinary skills and insights.

Another important thing about Moses as a leader: He was a man with a vision. Nowhere is that more evident than in the way he organized and set up a judicial system. What he did was revolutionary, far-reaching, and in some ways, a forerunner to the system we have today.

During his forty years in the wilderness, Moses constantly sought to demonstrate the difference between the sacred and the civil aspects of justice. This couldn't have been easy for a man who was forever shuffling between meetings with God and with his unruly, unhappy followers.

That Moses was able to walk such a tightrope, and do it successfully, is perhaps the greatest testament to his skills as a leader.

What Moses did was formulate a system that allowed certain pious elders to serve as judges. This was a bold and innovative move, one that demonstrated Moses' great cleverness and insight. Essentially, what this did was create an organization for the administration of justice, like our hierarchical system of courts, rather than giving all the power to a single judge. This splintering of authority may also have helped lead to the division of the Israelites into tribes, a development that would play a crucial role in the later history of the Jewish people.

In his capacity as leader, Moses was constantly having to be creative and daring. It's impossible for us to imagine the problems that arose during those forty years in the desert. The demands must have been endless. Almost certainly, Moses' patience was tested hourly.

Like most great leaders, Moses served many roles and wore many different hats. As the Israelites' deliverer from Egypt, he naturally became their leader. As the man who mediated between God and his covenant, he founded the community of Israel. As the interpreter of that covenant, he was Israel's first true legislator. And as the one who constantly interceded on behalf of his people, he became their priest.

In the pantheon of great leaders, none stands taller than Moses. And few are as appealing to us. We are drawn to him for many reasons, not the least of which is that, despite the myth-making of history, legends, and movies, despite all the miracles and wonders that surrounded him, he was first and foremost a human being. He didn't ask for the great burden that God placed on him and he didn't seek out the role of deliverer, but he accepted them and he succeeded against all odds. As a result, Moses gave rise to a mighty nation, hope to the despairing, and an ideal of freedom that lives to this day.

3

BUILD A TEAM EGO

In March of 1999 Bill Russell, one of the greatest basketball players in the history of the sport, and a man who once led the Celtics to eleven NBA championships in thirteen years, came to a Celtic game in the FleetCenter in Boston. Russell has been called the most successful team athlete in sports' history, so I asked him if he would speak to the team before the game. This was only minutes before the team had to go out on the floor to prepare for the game and Russell didn't have time to prepare. He just walked into the locker room and spoke off the cuff for twenty minutes.

The first thing he told the players was he was the most egotistical son of a bitch in the room. I was surprised. I always had seen Bill Russell as a very humble man. But then he added the qualifier, the addendum that made all the difference:

"But my ego always was a team ego," he said. "My ego was totally linked with the success of my team. It wasn't linked to personal achievement. It was linked to *team* achievement. And the greatest disappointment I had as a player was the year I was hurt and we didn't win a twelfth title."

You could see the players' reaction. Here was this man who is one of the greatest players in the history of the sport and he was telling them that the only thing that mattered to him was how his team did. That, to this day, his greatest professional regret were those two years the Celtics didn't win. Not his personal stats. Not how much money he made. Not how many endorsements he had, how many titles his team won. I knew then why Russell had been a great leader as well as a great player.

Great leaders inflate the people around them. Poor leaders deflate the people around them.

Everything you do as a leader should be geared to building "a team ego." It has to be right there in your mission statement, an integral part of your dreams and goals, a major part of your vision. Building team ego is essential, for team ego is the difference between being mediocre and being something special. You can be productive. You can be successful. You can be many positive things. But I don't think you truly can be great without team ego.

Russell also spoke to us about what it had meant to him be the Celtics' captain. "You don't understand how important that was for me," he said. "To me, I was a part of history."

But being there that day I knew that the players in that room didn't have the same feeling about the Celtics jersey that Russell had. They didn't have that strong sense of team ego.

I had prepped Russell on two things before he spoke. I told him that the players tended to think shot before pass, and offense before defense; that they invariably were too consumed with personal statistics and thinking about their next contract. I also told him that we essentially had a young team, one that had been crippled by its youth and inexperience.

He also knew who our young captain was—Antoine Walker. At the time Antoine was going through a difficult stretch, to the point that he was getting booed at home in the FleetCenter, often for taking what the fans perceived to be bad shots.

At one point, Russell pointed to Antoine and told the rest of the team, "This young man shoots all the time. I know people like that. He's not changing. It's up to you guys to get him good shots, so he doesn't shoot a poor percentage. It's up to you to do what you can do to help him. I always looked at how I could help my teammates be better. That's the difference between team ego and individual ego. My ego was centered around my team's accomplishments, not my accomplishments. That's the difference. Right now, your egos are individual and that is a problem to a team."

Russell was right on target. Individual ego is the poison pill and it's all around us in our culture. In sports, the measure of success is how much money you make, what stats you achieve, how many endorsements you get, how many individual accomplishments you can compile. In business, success is status. It's what kind of car you drive. What country club you belong to. How big your house is. Where your kids go to school. How much of a raise you've received. All of the accoutrements of contemporary life. And it's so pervasive that it's very difficult to fight against it.

A case in point:

Russell's speech to the team that night was very powerful. He is a charismatic man, with a definite presence, and there's no way a player could listen to his message that night and then go out and essentially play selfish basketball, thinking shot before pass, offense before defense, and the other ills that cripple a basketball team. That night we played unselfishly and there's no question that was the legacy of Russell's speech that night.

So this turned our season around, right? The players took Russell's message, made it an article of their collective faith, and played appreciably differently the rest of the season, right?

Well, not quite.

We soon reverted back to our old tricks, like someone with no sense of memory. Again, most of the players were back to thinking offense before defense, shot before pass, seeing the game in individual terms. In a sense, it was like Russell had never come into the locker room, had never given such a powerful speech.

Why? I think there are a couple of reasons.

The most obvious is that significant behavioral change is very difficult, something that takes more than one locker room speech to begin altering, no matter how powerful that speech is. As we discussed earlier, messages must be constantly repeated in a variety of ways. To expect my team to instantly shed all their bad habits and find maturity after one locker room speech by Bill Russell—even if it was a great one—would have been foolish. The second reason is that it illustrates just how powerful the forces of "me first" thinking are in the culture.

GROUNDING YOUR TEAM IN A GROUP CULTURE

How do you build "team ego"? First, you have to understand that this might just be the toughest job you have to do as a leader.

It's one thing to get an individual to perform better. You can appeal to that person's ego, her ambitions, her dreams. You can give her salary incentives. You can try to make her realize how fulfilling it ultimately will be for her to utilize her full potential. You can tell her how her life can be better in so many ways. But it's another to get individuals to see their ego in terms of the group, to get as much fulfillment from the group's success as they do from their own. Especially in an era that genuflects to the cult of individualism.

Building a team ego is what I'm trying to do with the Celtics and it's the hardest thing I've ever had to do in my career. I am trying to change attitudes, many of which have been all but chiseled in stone, and that kind of change takes time.

One of our problems is that we don't have a leader right now. Our veteran players are quiet, laid-back guys whose nature is not to be leaders, while our young players are leaders only when they are playing well. That's not leadership. Anyone can lead the league in high fives when things are going well. But during adversity, those times when things are not going well, is when you need leaders in your group. And young people—in a losing environment—tend not to be leaders. Instead, they tend to think in terms of self. So this is when you need positive people more than ever, because they inflate the attitude of a deflated team.

This was not so vital when I was coaching in college, because in college the basketball coach is the unquestioned leader, his influence all-pervasive. In the pros, however, players need peer pressure, too. Groups that have strong leadership within have a decided advantage. That's why I'm such a fan of Kevin Garnett, the great young player of the Minnesota Timberwolves. Even though he didn't go to college, and is still very young, he has emerged as the undisputed leader of that team, someone who gets everyone around him to play hard.

If you look at the great NBA teams of the past fifteen years, one of the common threads is they all had great veteran leaders within the group: Larry Bird with the Celtics; Magic Johnson with the Lakers; Isiah Thomas, Rick Mahorn, and Bill Laimbeer with the Pistons; Michael Jordan with the Bulls. Each one had his own style, but they all demanded excellence from the people around them. Not just once in a while, not just when things were going good for them, but all the time.

You can find differences in their respective styles. There's the famous story about how Bird called his teammates "sissies" in a press conference after a playoff loss. This was a "no no" when it came to Celtic tradition and there was some speculation that it would backfire. It didn't. In fact, it was just the opposite. It worked. Bird's teammates responded and the Celtics won the next game.

As a leader, these are the kind of qualities that you always have to be looking for in the people you hire or pick for your organization, these leadership traits that often are just as important as talent:

● Who are the people who put the group first?
● Who will subordinate their own individual interests for the common good?

● Who will sacrifice?
● What is a person's emotional intelligence?

In the long run, this might be just as important as their IQ. When you hire a person it's almost as if you are marrying them. You must know as much about them as possible. How are they going to react in times of adversity? How committed to the success of the group are they? These questions are just as important as how talented a person is. If you continually hire people who don't have these traits you eventually will pay the price.

You need people around you who share the same values you do, people who are going to be your messengers. Because it can't just be you all the time. So you need the manager, the department head, the supervisor, those people who are going to spread your message. For, more and more, people tend to think of themselves as free agents, always looking for the best deal, especially in a business climate that's often about downsizing and change. Once upon a time it was common for people to work for the same company all their working life—along with the loyalty that's implied there—but now that's changed. As a leader, you must give loyalty. But you can't expect it back.

Take Ron Mercer, for example:

There were people who said to me that because I once had recruited Ron to come to Kentucky, and that the Celtics had been his first team in the NBA, he might take less money to stay with the Celtics when his contract was up. Not true. Not in today's climate. And this is not intended as a knock on Ron. It's simply the way it is: In most cases, people's primary allegiance is to themselves and what they believe is the best deal they can get for themselves. This is not exactly the best climate for building team ego, but as a leader in professional basketball the window of opportunity is very small.

Still, this must be your goal.

One of the things I did with the Celtics during the 1998–'99 season was to get my players to listen to Bob Cousy and Tom

Heinsohn talk about the old days on their telecasts, reminiscences about when the Celtics were the best team in basketball. They are both former Celtic greats and they both broadcast our games on the road: Heinsohn all the time, Cousy once in a while. The more Heinsohn and Cousy are around our players, the more they talk about what winning meant to them, what it still means to them even after so many years. All this is vitally important to the maturation of a young team. Cousy and Heinsohn are living examples of the mind-set we want our players to reach, the belief that everything is subordinate to winning. Like the time Heinsohn told a great story about Bill Russell. Seems the Celtics were losing and Russell—who was playing the best of anyone—came into the huddle and asked, "What can I do better to help us win this game? How can I best help?"

These kind of stories are invaluable. To learn from people who have come before is essential and leaders must constantly be stressing that to the people they're leading.

This is a lesson I learned as a kid. In high school and college I spent several summers at the Five Star basketball camp in Pennsylvania where, at an impressionable age, I was exposed to many coaches, most of whom gave talks to the campers. I saw how some were very good, and some weren't so good, and it really had little to do with what they were talking about. It was their style. Jim Lynam, who went on to coach the Washington Bullets, was very good at doing the individual drills about which he was always speaking. He could still play and he used his basketball ability to his advantage. Marv Kessler was very funny. Hubie Brown, who later went on to coach both the Atlanta Hawks and the New York Knicks and is now a commentator on TNT, had an amazing presence. He used his voice and his presentation to command respect, injecting everything with a big dose of passion. If he sensed he was losing the kids' attention he would stop and make them all stand up and stretch. He simply refused not to have people listen to him.

I saw how they all used these motivational strengths. So

when my turn came to give a lecture I tried to use some of these same techniques, to incorporate them into my approach.

I had a basic fear of failure, so I would look at others who weren't so successful. Why had they failed? What had they done wrong? Why did the kids seem to turn them off?

I also saw how willing all of the coaches at Five Star were to pass on their expertise, as if each one had a gift that they were happy to pass on. As though they all wanted the kids at the camp to both excel and to become part of the culture of basketball. It was as though somehow, some way, the camp had developed its own team ego, one that benefited everyone that came into contact with it.

That is the climate I'm trying to create around the Celtics, this feeling that the players can learn from those who made the journey before them. It's the one lesson all great teams have to tell us. If you read about great teams, and the people who played for them, the two themes that connect all of them is 1) the team eventually became bigger than all the individuals who played for it, and 2) the players ultimately realized that playing for a great team was the best experience in their professional lives.

The 1998 New York Yankees are an example of that.

That was the great Yankee team that won an astounding 114 games during the regular season, culminating in a World Series title. But who was the star of that team? Was it Derek Jeter, the shortstop? Was it Bernie Williams, the center fielder? Was it pitchers David Wells and David Cone? Was it Paul O'Neill? Tino Martinez? Was it Scott Brosius, who had such a great World Series? Was manager Joe Torre the true star, somehow able to blend all these great talents into a cohesive unit, doing this in the toughest city to manage, in the unrelenting eye of the New York media? Who was the real star?

The answer?

None of them. Not really. A case can be made that none of them were even the best at their position in the American

League that particular year. Yet they were integral parts of a great group, their individual talents blending together to form something so much greater than what they ever could have done individually.

That's the lesson I'm trying to impart to my young Celtics team and it's more difficult than you might think.

Why? Because I am just one voice.

One voice in a cacophony of voices, all of which essentially give out a different message. Think about it for a second. From advertising to popular culture, from families to friends, people are constantly being told to look out for themselves. This is difficult to battle against, for in a sense you always are swimming against the tide. Anything you can do to try and battle this onslaught is good.

For instance, the New Jersey Nets brought Anthony Robbins, a renowned motivational speaker, to speak to the Nets players. I found this to be very curious. How will the majority of today's NBA players relate to Anthony Robbins? Cousy and Heinsohn, on the other hand, both were great players. They played on championship Celtic teams. They achieved what our players still hope to one day achieve. So even though they're older and of a different generation, our players would be foolish not to listen to them, to learn from them.

That's important.

Because I can't be the only voice they ever hear. Eventually, people will simply get tired of listening to you and your voice will become little more than some whine they always hear in their sleep, some noise to be turned down. Eventually, people will tune you out. Especially young people, many of whom don't listen very well anyway. Again, your gratification cannot come from having people hang on your every word. It comes from winning, from being successful, and especially from knowing you were able to help a group of people work together to achieve their best.

VEST PEOPLE IN THE PROCESS

One of the ways I built team ego at Providence College in the mid eighties was to convince the players that they were the hardest-working team in college basketball and to take tremendous pride in that.

I was inheriting a team with a poor record, a college program that had known little success since the Big East Conference had started six years earlier. Naturally, the players had a very low collective self-esteem. So it would have been ridiculous for me to come in with a little pep talk and tell them that things were fine, that all they had to do was maintain the status quo. That would surely have been a prelude to disaster. Nor could I tell them that we were going to rely on our natural ability, because by any standard of measure Providence was one of the least talented teams in the Big East.

My approach instead was to give them something they could cling to, something that could make them begin to feel good about themselves. That something was our work ethic. We were going to work harder than any other college basketball team in the country and that was going to be the badge we showed to the rest of the basketball world. We were going to ride our work ethic as far as it could possibly take us.

We did that. Now were we the hardest-working college basketball team in the country? Who knows. There are a lot of hard-working teams.

The point is *we believed* we were. That became our team ego. That became our source of pride and it totally changed our collective self-esteem. That team ego continued to grow as the season went on, was the reason we overachieved to the point that we eventually went to the Final Four, a complete turnaround from two years earlier.

At Kentucky, we had a different problem. The year we won the national championship we probably had too many talented players. The challenge then was not only to try to get them all playing time, but to convince the players that all of them would benefit by the team winning the national championship.

One of the ways we did this was to constantly praise—both publicly and privately—players for subordinating their individual interest for the sake of the team. Any time someone did this it was immediately recognized and reinforced. As a coaching staff, we never allowed this to take place without notice. Just the opposite. If I thought Antoine Walker, a sophomore at the time, had played unselfishly, even if he hadn't scored a lot of points, I would publicly point this out and commend him. As a coaching staff, we constantly praised people who were sacrificing their individual goals for the collective goal of the group. And as we started to win, the momentum growing, this became easier.

Doing this in the workplace where you don't have the potential of a winning headline for motivation is obviously more difficult. People have their own lives, their own families, and work is just part of their lives. Yet people spend a large part of their day in the workplace. They want to be successful. They want to be happy in the workplace. They want to feel fulfilled, that they are utilizing their full potential. They want to believe that all the hours they spend at work are worth it. They want to feel that they're an important part of something great. It's your job to help them get there.

* * *

Leaders must also show generosity. You can't be frugal. You must find some way to share the wealth. For instance, when a CEO gets a five-million-dollar bonus he should immediately take one million of that and give it to the people who also should be rewarded for their contribution to the result that led to the bonus.

This does two things: It reinforces the notion that everyone benefits when the organization does well and it further develops team ego.

One of the things I did in the summer of 1998 was to get

several members of my staff to lose weight as part of a physical fitness kick. We were coming out of the "lockout year," a year in which our players had not reported to training camp in the best of shape and I wanted this year to be different. So by having our staff involved in physical fitness I figured not only would this raise their self-esteem, but also send a message to everyone that we, as an organization, were very concerned about fitness.

When they came back in September, ten of them had lost between twenty and thirty pounds, and I told them to keep it off until Christmas. At Christmas, I gave them them a hundred dollars for every pound they had lost. Nine of them collected.

Again, this is a small example of building team ego. It shows those members of my staff that I care about them as people, not just employees. It's a subtle message to the players that we, as an organization, are committed to physical fitness; that we, as a group, are going to be in great shape. It contributes to team ego.

A leader must be generous with her wealth, with her time, with her listening, with her problem solving, with everything. To be a truly great leader you must give of yourself. You can't be selfish. You must convey a vision of partnership, that you not only care about the people who work for you, but that it's important they're successful, too.

This concept of partnership can't be stressed enough. It can't just be about you, your career, your success. The people you are leading must know that they have a vested interest in the organization, that their careers are important, too; that they also will be rewarded for their hard work. I am very proud of the fact that eleven of my former assistant coaches went on to become head coaches. That was my vision for them.

Leaders must understand that they are being watched and evaluated by their employees, too. How you, as a leader, respond to your boss will often determine how your employees deal with you. How you take orders from your boss often will determine how people will take orders from you.

Case in point:

I take orders from Paul Gaston, the principle owner of the Celtics. He is my boss. Now if I bitch and moan and complain about Paul, the people I'm leading invariably will do the same thing with me. They invariably will follow my lead. If I take orders in a professional way, the odds are so will they. Jim O'Brien, one of my assistant coaches with the Celtics, sets an excellent example. He takes orders in a very positive way and this sets the tone for everyone else on the staff.

The people you're leading will take their cues from you. If you are organized, they will tend to be organized. If you have a great work ethic, so will they. If you are positive and upbeat, those traits will be more prevalent in your workplace. You set the tone.

The mistake many executive make is that they believe that money solves all ills. If they pay their employees good salaries, they feel that's enough and that everyone should be satisfied.

Not so.

In his book *1001 Ways to Reward Employees*, Bob Nelson explains that money isn't everything to employees; that few management concepts are as solidly rooted as the one that says positive reinforcement—rewarding behavior you want repeated—works. In fact, in today's business climate, rewards and recognition are more important than ever.

"Studies indicate that employees find personal recognition more motivational than money," Nelson writes. There are many ways to do this, certainly, but one rule is standard: These programs should be highly public, whether it's giving out rewards or something as easy as writing a thank-you memo.

I long ago learned that publicly acknowledging the people who don't get a lot of the limelight does wonders for team morale. You must make these people know you not only are aware of their efforts, you appreciate them. No team can be successful without the people who come and work hard every day in practice, yet don't get much playing time in the games. No group can be successful without the input from the myriad number of behind-the-scenes people, the support staff that often makes organizations work. These people must be publicly recognized and rewarded for their efforts in front of their peers. You can do this at meetings or at business functions by simply stating their names and contributions and a heartfelt thank you. The action is simple, but the employees' gratitude will be profound.

These awards, Nelson contends, should be both informal and formal. He also says that simply asking for employee input is a motivational tool. He makes four references to companies who go out of their way to single out outstanding employees, whether it was employees at Apple Computer who worked on the first Macintosh who had their names listed on the inside of the computer; to the city of Philadelphia, which used an electronic message board on the side of a city skyscraper to honor the head of the local school system; to Mary Kay Cosmetics, which gives flowers to all secretaries during Secretaries' Week. Nelson also writes about the Minnesota Department of Natural Resources, which, polling its employees, discovered that 68 percent of the respondents said it was important to realize their work was appreciated by others.

You can't overlook this. You must always be trying to reaffirm the belief that the group is significant. For if it's perceived not to be, then why should someone have any real allegiance to it?

One thing we do at the Celtics is show a video before all our home games as part of our pregame introductions. It's a quick, capsule summary of the franchise's great history, a montage of images flashed before the crowd in a darkened arena. And, sure, it's for our fans, a brief reminder of the Celtics' great history, as are the championship banners that hang in the rafters, the tradition we want our fans to hook up to as soon as they enter the FleetCenter. It's also for our players, too, a nightly reminder that they're part of something important, something that transcends them as individuals. And though it's safe to say that many of our current players couldn't tell you much about the specifics of the Celtics' history, the inherent message is: You're not just playing for any NBA franchise; you're playing for one of the greatest franchises in the history of sports.

You see this all the time in sports.

The Purple People Eaters of the old Minnesota Vikings, the Steel Curtain of the old Pittsburgh Steelers, the Dallas Cowboys and their America's Team image; these nicknames ultimately began to take on a life of their own, an identity, and the players were obviously taking great pride in them. These are all examples of team ego, the particular group being more significant than the individual players.

So many of the great sports teams have this, whether it's the storied college basketball programs of North Carolina, UCLA, Duke, and Kentucky or other sports legends like the New York Yankees and Montreal Canadiens; this feeling that the players come and go, but the organization lives on forever, greater than all the individuals can ever be. It's what all the great organizations have, from Coca-Cola and IBM to Disney.

And while it obviously takes years to acquire this kind of status, there are little things you can do to help speed up the process. It can be the uniforms. It can be the locker room. It can be the training table. It can be how well lit the parking lot is. How the quality of the food in the cafeteria is. How clean the restrooms are. It can be ergonomic furniture. It can be the presence of new technology on every desk. It can be a good rug on the floor instead of a cheap carpet. It can be anything that shows people that the workplace is first class, designed to make their work lives better.

All these things send out messages to the people you are leading, even if some of them are subtle. Not only must the workplace be some place people want to come to, but everything also must be geared to creating an environment that's the essence of professionalism, a place where success can flourish.

That's what the Celtics had in the era in which Bill Russell played, the very real sense that the players were a part of something far greater than themselves, part of a wonderful history that was documented in all those championship banners hanging from the rafters. That was the essence of Russell's speech to my team back in the winter of 1999, the key ingredient in what the Celtics had been able to accomplish during those glory days.

CREATE AN UNSELFISH TEAM

I was once brought into a Wall Street firm to speak to a select group of their employees, fourteen in all. These fourteen people were all achievers, the best salespeople in the firm. They all made big money for the firm. But there was a problem:

They all, in their own ways, belittled other people in the firm. They either put them down or showed in other ways that they didn't respect them, to the point that it had become a problem to the firm, extremely disruptive and counterproductive.

The first thing I did was ask them two questions:

Are you ever cynical?

Are you ever moody?

And you know what the response was? All fourteen of them said no. Not only did they fail to admit their behavior, they didn't even think they were exhibiting these negative qualities.

This is not surprising. Many people, when told that their attitude in the workplace is destructive, will not believe it, especially if they're achievers. They don't see any connection between the two.

I had one Celtic employee who was infamous for treating people poorly. Everyone had difficulties with him, yet when I confronted him with this he was flabbergasted. He even countered by saying that dealing with people was one of his strengths.

You must understand, therefore, that not only will some people refuse to admit their weaknesses, often they don't even know they have them.

After the Wall Street guys had said that, in their minds, they weren't cynical and they didn't belittle people, I asked them two more questions:

What are you doing to make the people around you better?

What are you doing to make your team better?

None of them had any answers.

"That's your biggest weakness," I told them. "You don't recognize team potential. You think that as long as you're doing great, you're producing, things are fine. You are the equivalent of the basketball player who feels good about himself when he scores twenty-five points, even if the team loses."

It's my constant message to my team: The true mark of greatness is making the people around you better, elevating them.

Those are the people in sports that we remember as greats. It's not the ones with the great individual achievements as much as those who were able to lead their teams to great victories. According to countless magazine articles and several books, both Bird and Jordan did it through the fear factor. They both worked so hard and wanted to win so much that they had no tolerance for others they perceived not to want to win badly enough. They would ridicule teammates in practice who they didn't feel were working hard enough, producing enough. They would attack them publicly, as well as privately, until those teammates changed. You couldn't be selfish around Bird or Jordan. Nor could you coast. They simply wouldn't let you.

Russell did it a different way.

He was so team-oriented it rubbed off on everyone around him. Here was the most dominant player in the game, but he was clearly oblivious to personal statistics. There's a great story about the famous playoff game against Philadelphia in the sixties, the one in which John Havlicek stole the in-bounds pass in the game's dying seconds to preserve the Celtics' victory, one of the prized moments in Celtics history. What's largely been forgotten is that Russell's in-bounds pass had hit one of the guide wires right before that, giving Philadelphia the ball back.

As the story goes, Russell came back to the huddle after the ill-fated pass and said to his teammates, "If you guys don't bail me out, I'm going to be the goat of this game. You guys have to bail me out."

He understood they were all in it together, that they needed one another.

Another great Russell story is the time he bet Wilt Chamberlain that he was going to average twenty points in the upcoming season, a bet that started when Chamberlain chided him that averaging twenty points was the barometer. Russell countered by saying he could average anything he wanted.

But a funny thing happened. When training camp started, Russell realized that, sure, he could average twenty points for the year and win the bet, but to do so would make the Celtics a worse team. He realized the Celtics had enough scorers, and if he tried to score more it would only upset the team's chemistry. So Russell went the other way that year. He scored less and the Celtics won another NBA championship.

However they did it, though, Bird, Jordan, and Russell all understood team ego.

My Kentucky team understood this in 1996, the year we won the national championship.

But it took a while for them to learn it.

That was an incredibly talented college team, one I feel that, defensively, was one of the best in college basketball in the past twenty-five years. Eight players on that team eventually went on to play in the NBA. The problem for me, then, was how to keep them all happy in an age when so many young players are so stats-conscious, so individually driven? How do you get people to subordinate their individual agendas when they all had big goals and dreams?

In the middle of the year, even though we were winning, I could sense the problems starting. Whether it was the body language after the games or the attitude in practice, I knew there were too many guys getting down because of their poor individual stats or thinking they were playing too few minutes. So we had a meeting.

"I can't, in any way, satisfy your egos," I told them. "I don't have enough basketballs. I don't have enough minutes. I don't have enough stats. I don't have enough of the things that make you happy. I can't satisfy your egos, but I can satisfy your dreams. Whether that's to play in the NBA or win a national championship. And if you win the national championship you will get your individual reputations. In the end you will be judged by winning."

At that point Antoine Walker got up to speak. He was a sophomore at the time.

"Everyone knows I'm the most selfish guy on this team," he said. "But I don't want this to go the other way. I will do anything to make this team win."

After that meeting, our common goal was simple: We would say things to help one another. We would do things to help one another.

That was the day we found team ego, as we left that meeting one step closer to the national championship.

And without team ego you cannot win.

This is the message I'm forever giving to my Celtics team, the same one I gave to those fourteen Wall Street hotshots: You all have the money, so now what? What do you do next?

The answer is to strive for greatness.

I point out to them that no one really remembers the great basketball players of the past that did not win championships. No one talks about Elvin Hayes and Bob McAdoo, who certainly were great players. They talk about the people who won.

In the 1999 season my Celtics team was the antithesis of team ego. We were governed by individual ego, so when we had adversity we resorted to the things individuals do when they have little invested in the group. The players blamed one another. They complained that not enough plays were being run for them. We had guy who complained about the kind of warm-up drills we ran.

Groups with strong group ego don't do that.

Which is why they have a chance to win.

One of the things I did this past year was to get pictures of former NBA greats to put on the walls of the locker room. Not pictures of these players in their prime, but as they are now. The message to my players? These guys are you in twenty-five or thirty years. They are remembered because they won. That's their slice of immortality. Not how much money they made as individuals, not how many points they scored, but that they won.

For in the end you are judged by winning.

Nothing more.

Your job as a leader is to constantly reinforce that.

KEY CHAPTER POINTS

● **Grounding Your Team in a Group Culture** This is the toughest job you have to do as a leader, especially in this age of rampant individualism. But this is what all the great organizations have accomplished.

● **Vest People in the Process** People have to know that they are an integral part of the group and that their success and the group's success is one and the same.

● **Create an Unselfish Team** People must be made to understand that true greatness is not only being productive yourself, but elevating the people around you, making them better.

BILL RUSSELL

Bill Russell was named the Most Valuable Player of the NBA five times.

But that is not why he is remembered as one of the greatest players in the history of basketball.

He is remembered that way because he is the most successful athlete in the history of team sports, having won eleven world championships in twelve years as the center for the Boston Celtics. This came on the heels of winning two NCAA titles in college at the University of San Francisco and being the cornerstone of a U.S. Olympic team that won a gold medal in 1956.

Was all this winning just a coincidence?

Hardly.

It was a result of Russell's belief in winning as the ultimate form of athletic expression and his awareness at a relatively young age that, in order to best give his team a chance to win, he had to subordinate some of his individual goals. It is this awareness that runs all through Russell's career, his realization that being a leader meant doing the most he could do to ensure his team's success.

It's a realization he talks about in his memoir, *Second Wind*. "In order to win you have to get yourself past a lot of things that may not be vital to winning but make you feel good, like scoring points," he writes.

It was a lesson he first learned as a sophomore at the University of San Francisco. That was his breakthrough year as a basketball player, the year, he writes, "I decided I was going to be a great basketball player." The epiphany happened at half-time early in the season in a game in Provo, Utah, when, after challenged at halftime by his coach, he went out for the second half and "everything inside me poured itself into that decision, all the anger and wonder joined together."

Russell became a dominant player that year.

"But I couldn't have cared less about the coach or any of the other players. At the end of the season I looked up and saw that we made a mediocre record of 14–7 even though we had enough talent to be one of the best teams in the country."

Russell never forget that lesson, never forgot his sopho-more year at San Francisco when the team was riddled with dis-sension. "I was part of it. I was not strong enough to change the atmosphere for the better and the team wasn't strong enough to change me, so we feuded."

After that season, he vowed to never again concentrate on individual goals at the expense of the team. He had learned how important team chemistry was, a lesson he took with him throughout the rest of his career. It also colored his attitudes about individual honors in what is so clearly a team sport, a sport in which success depends upon everyone's individual games blending together to form a more powerful whole.

That's why Russell enjoyed playing with the Celtics so much, for they were the very definition of *team*. The Celtics, during the Russell years, were the epitome of team. Everyone had their roles; everyone was comfortable with their roles. More importantly, the sum of the individual roles added up to the best whole in the game.

Russell admits that when he first entered the pros he had a very limited offensive game, with little confidence in his shoot-ing ability.

"But I did think I could help win games," he writes, "and that's what I tried to concentrate on. Everything else would fol-low." Russell also said that the Celtics—along with their leg-endary coach Red Auerbach—understood what it took to win.

They understood that if everyone was always trying to score they would not be as good, so they concentrated on what they did well, and it was that combination of skills that made the Celtics a great team, even though there were other teams in that era that might have had more scorers. It is Russell's contention that the Celtics came to care more about winning than anything else, and that was rare.

"One of the first things Red told me when I joined the team," he writes in *Second Wind*, "was that he was counting on me to get the ball to (Bob) Cousy or (Bill) Sharman for the fast break. This, plus defense, was to be my fundamental role on the team, and as long as I performed these functions well he would never pressure me to score more points. He also promised that he would never discuss statistics in salary negotiations.

"This one conversation accomplished as much as a whole season's worth of tactical coaching. It showed me that Red knew what he was talking about; he was asking me to do what I did best and at the same time what the Celtics needed most. In addition, he removed a lot of the pressure I felt about scoring more. All that was to the good. If he'd said to me, 'What we need from you is twenty-five points a game,' I might have been able to do that, but we wouldn't have won much."

4

ACT WITH INTEGRITY

You must always speak the truth.

This must be a fundamental part of any leadership style, at the cornerstone of your philosophy. You can lead in a variety of ways and you can debate the efficacy of the variety of methods that can be used to reach your goals, but the need for integrity is irrefutable.

We've all seen many examples of how vagueness and a lack of trust can not only create problems, but can cause minor problems to grow into major ones.

Let's take a look at President Clinton, for example:

By many standards of measure he's been a great president. The economy is great. He has kept us out of war. We have low unemployment. The deficit has been reduced. Times have been good. Yet his presidency will go down as somewhat tarnished, when it shouldn't have been.

Why? Because of a lack of integrity that the public perceived.

Unfortunately, at the present time, this is how he will be remembered. Not for the job he did in the White House. Not for his accomplishments, considerable as they may be, but for the scandals that have tarnished his career and complicated everything. At this juncture in time only history will tell us how he'll be judged as a president.

You must act and speak honestly. This is a prerequisite for any leadership position, one of the articles of your faith. When you lie—or tell a mistruth—you only create bigger problems for yourself. The problems only deepen, get worse. Telling the truth is the best problem-solver there is. Lying makes a problem part of the future; truth makes a problem part of the past.

A strong sense of integrity is near the top of any list of pre-requisites to be a leader. Cutting corners, bending rules, and the use of situational ethics may get results in the short term, but they eventually will undermine any leadership style. They are the problems that eat away at any organization, for inherent in any leadership situation is the belief that the leader is going to tell the truth.

When the president addresses the American people, isn't there the belief that he's going to tell us the truth? Wouldn't we react differently if there was a disclaimer on the television screen that what the president says when he addresses the American people might not always be the truth? Isn't the first thing anyone does in a court of law in this country is to swear to tell the truth?

Isn't that what we want from our leaders?

Isn't that what we have a right to expect?

Nothing will turn people against you quicker than to be per-ceived as dishonest. People will forgive you if you make mis-takes. You can have errors in judgment. You can slip up in a variety of ways, but you can't be dishonest. That will only create an environment in your organization that eventually will rot from within.

Look at the great leaders of history and one of the common traits is integrity, believing and sticking to principles. From George Washington, whose famous saying is "I would never tell a lie," to Franklin Roosevelt, who began one of his famous fire-side chats by saying there is no good news to report this evening, to Martin Luther King Jr., who marched through the South for his principles; we admire people who not only believe in things, but stand up for them. There is the sense that these people believed in things that transcended their own individual advancement, believed in things that helped the people they were leading.

Isn't that was true leadership is?

Isn't that what we want from our leaders?

We don't follow leaders because we want them to one day have the opportunity to move into a bigger house. We don't follow leaders because we necessarily want to see them do well. We follow leaders who hook us with their vision, who convince us they can make our lives better. We follow leaders whom we know we can trust.

In *Lincoln on Leadership*, author Donald T. Phillips writes about how the perception of honesty was at the root of Lincoln's popularity, of how the moniker "Honest Abe" was used in the presidential election in 1860 and was a major component of the Republican campaign strategy. Lincoln was perceived to be "one of the common people, a railsplitter from Illinois who was honest beyond question." Phillips also contends Lincoln was as honest as he was purported to be and it was this honesty that made him a great leader.

According to Phillips, Lincoln constantly stressed two concepts that over the years have mobilized Americans: "the pursuit of liberty" and "equality." In short, his integrity became the nation's integrity.

"Lincoln always did the right thing, or at least he attempted to," Phillips writes. "Even though he had some detractors, Lincoln attained success, admiration, and a positive image by maintaining his integrity and honesty. . . . Emulating his style will earn leaders the trust and respect that ultimately foster passionate commitment. This approach shows that the truth is a common denominator for all interactions, among any group, and with people of varying personalities."

If you are delivering bad news to the group you are leading, speaking the truth can be the best tool you have. Telling the truth—whether it's about layoffs or poor fiscal results or something else—keeps the message free of politics, free from "hidden meaning" as much as possible to the employees. The truth is useful to convey *any* message you have, actually, that people may not be prepared for.

When I went to Kentucky in the spring of 1989, the number one priority was to restore the integrity of the basketball program, one that had been embarrassed by recruiting violations that resulted in NCAA probation. This was more important than winning games. More important than recruiting players. More important than filling up Rupp Arena. We had to erase the tarnish from Kentucky's name. I was forever walking into athletic director C. M. Newton's office and telling him we had to report ourselves over some violation of the rules, no matter how minor it might have been. We always were self-reporting ourselves. Anytime I found something wrong I went to C.M. and told him what had happened and how I had handled it. I kept him abreast of everything.

There was no gray area. We didn't have that luxury at Kentucky. We had to do things by the strict letter of the rules. We had to restore Kentucky's good name and the only way to do that was to be totally committed to building a program that had the highest integrity. There could be no more bending of the rules, no more operating in some gray area, for there always were going to be people who weren't going to believe things were different, people who still were going to believe it was business as usual at Kentucky. We had to build a program that had absolute integrity and I had to be strong enough not to allow anything to tarnish that.

DO THE RIGHT THING

My Kentucky experience taught me the value of integrity as part of any leadership style. Everything you do, everything you say, is under a magnifying glass. You no longer are representing only yourself. You also are representing the organization you are leading and that changes everything.

As the face of an organization, you are going to be second-guessed, examined in ways you never were before. This simply goes with the territory. And you must realize you're not going to get the benefit of the doubt. We live in very cynical times and people often will believe the rumors, think the worst. People are going to always be judging you, lying in the weeds waiting for you to slip up. You can't afford to give them that opportunity. So it's imperative that you act and speak honestly.

Take Jim Harrick, for example.

In 1995 he won the national collegiate basketball championship as the coach at UCLA. In a sense that was his dream job and Harrick was someone who had paid a lot of coaching dues before he got it. In many ways, it was a wonderful coaching story, a guy who had spent years in the game's bushes and finally got all the way to the top of the mountain. A year and a half later, shortly before the start of the season, he was fired.

Why?

It was reported that he lied to his athletic director about an expense account. He had taken a group of people to dinner and two of them were players of his—which is a minor NCAA violation. To get around this, Harrick substituted the names of two other people instead.

In the grand scheme of things, what Harrick did was nothing major, at least not in the light of some of the things that go on in the world of collegiate athletics. You could even make a case that Harrick didn't deserve to be fired over that incident. But the truth was, the most important thing to the UCLA athletic director was that Harrick had lied to him, and because of that, it cost Jim Harrick, a terrific coach and good person, one of the most prestigious jobs in all of college sports.

That's a good lesson for anyone.

It's easy to bend the rules, to exist in the gray area. People do it all the time in a variety of ways, whether it's driving over the speed limit, fudging on their taxes, trying to get free tickets for something, or telling little white lies to occasionally step around the truth. We've all undoubtedly done these things at one time or another. Often, they are nothing major and are done with no repercussions. But as a leader you always must be vigilant, for not only are you always under a microscope, but you also will be judged more harshly if things go public. Everything you do will be magnified simply because of your leadership position, even things that seem inconsequential.

For example:

One day I went to get a haircut in Boston, in a place on Newbury Street. I was very pleased with the haircut, but when I went to pay, the owner said, "No, Coach, I can't take your money."

That made me uncomfortable.

I told him that I really liked the job he'd done and I really wanted to come back in the future, but if he wouldn't let me pay I simply wasn't going to come back. My rule is simple: If I don't deserve it, I don't take it.

Now someone might say that was overreacting, but I don't think so.

This is not to say that I haven't taken things I really didn't deserve in the past. When I was a young coach at Boston University we used to go to a local pub after games and we rarely paid for anything. Certainly, there have been many times in my life when I accepted various perks that I didn't deserve. My point here is not to portray myself as a paragon of virtue, but you have to understand that the more visible your role is the more you must examine your own behavior.

What you're trying to do is to establish a code of conduct, a belief system you want those you lead to buy into. By taking things you haven't earned, accepting freebies that are being offered because of your position, you are compromising yourself. Maybe not in significant ways. Maybe not in ways that are going to affect your leadership style or have any impact on the people you are leading, but you are compromising yourself nonetheless. That's the bottom line here, not the fact that you can rationalize your behavior.

It's so much easier not to enter this gray ethical area in the first place. That's the mistake that's so easy to make, this sense that simply because you're in a leadership situation you're entitled to certain perks that other people don't get. You are not. And if you behave like you do, you can count on there being a backlash. People resent leaders who act imperially. People resent leaders who act as if they are royalty.

Acting like royalty flies in the face of jumping in the boat with the people you are leading. Acting imperially has the potential to sabotage everything you are trying to accomplish.

As a leader, you can't be taking. You have to always be giving.

Never forget that you're the one establishing the organization's tone. If you are perceived as someone who is always taking freebies and other perks, odds are that this will be the environment: one in which everyone will be looking for what he or she can get. That's just human nature.

This is true especially in this day and age in which the cult of individualism is so prevalent. Anything you do that supports this philosophy — even subconsciously — is an impediment to what you're trying to build. So if you are creating an atmosphere where the rules are treated loosely and the unofficial operating premise is essentially "me first," that's the environment with which you eventually will end up.

Another important aspect of honesty is being honest with yourself.

This is not always easy. For example, let's look at this story with Ron Mercer. After the 1999 season I sat down with Mercer—who was about to enter the last year on his contract—and made him an offer the Celtics could afford. Without question, he could get more on the open market. I probably could have gone up 10 percent from my original offer, but it was apparent Ron wanted 80 percent more than what I could give him.

Then he asked me this question:

"Coach," he said, "you always say that you're my friend, but would you advise me to take this offer?"

"That's difficult to answer," I said.

He asked me if I would have taken the Celtics job if it had been for the same amount of money I was making at Kentucky?

I told him I left Kentucky for the Celtics for the challenge.

"Coach, would you have taken the challenge for the same amount of money?"

I told Ron that I would not have taken the Celtics job for the same amount of money, and I knew—at that point—that Ron Mercer's future was not going to be with the Celtics.

That night, I went home and realized I was a hypocrite. Yes, I had taken the Celtics job for the challenge, that the idea of trying to get the Celtics from fifteen wins to another championship banner excited me. Yes, it was time I needed another challenge in my life. Yes, the idea of having started my coaching career at Boston University and returning to coach the Celtics certainly appealed to me.

But who was I kidding?

I would not have taken the Celtics job unless the money had been significantly more than it had been at Kentucky. Until Ron Mercer questioned me, I was not being honest with myself.

PICK YOUR BATTLES

I want the Boston Celtics to have cheerleaders and a dance team, like so many of the other NBA teams have. I believe that in today's market, when you're asking someone to pay as much as a hundred dollars a ticket to come to an NBA game, you must make it as entertaining as possible. Not just on the court, but the entire evening, because in today's world you are competing with all the other options for someone's entertainment dollar. Therefore, you must always be trying to make the night as festive as possible. I feel cheerleaders and dance teams help in this regard. But Paul Gaston, the owner of the Celtics, Celtic patriarch Red Auerbach, and most of the Boston media do not want cheerleaders and dance teams. They say that these are not part of the Celtics tradition.

So what do I do? Do I tell them that although the Celtics hierarchy and media might not want them, a large percentage of the fans seem to? Do I try and demand that they see my way of thinking? Do I fight them over this?

No, I do not.

You can't take the Douglas MacArthur approach, can't be the autocratic, rigid leader. As a leader you want to build bridges for people to cross together, not burn them. You don't want to always be drawing lines in the sand, ones that you're constantly trying to defend. You don't square off over a dance team. What's that book title say? *Don't sweat the small stuff*? That book title is correct. You don't fight battles over peripheral issues. You fight battles over principles.

For example:

Antoine Walker takes a lot of criticism for his so-called wiggle after he makes a big basket, his little personal dance. He sees it as a form of personal expression, something that he says juices him up. Many people view it as showboating, an unnecessary affectation.

Often, I'm asked why don't I tell Antoine to knock it off, forbid him to do his "wiggle." So why don't I? Because I view it as a peripheral issue, not something that's worth fighting with Antoine about. The way I view it, I get on Antoine for his poor shot selection or for his lack of rebounding. I get on him when I think he's too heavy or is not working on his body diligently enough. There are the important things, not whether he does a little dance after a big basket. Do I wish he would forget about the "wiggle"? Yes. I don't think it necessarily helps his image, but I'm not going to make it an issue.

This is a lesson that took me a long time to learn.

When you're younger there often seems to be an incredible importance placed on having people do things your way, as if this somehow validates you. At least that's the way it was with me when I was younger. I was often so intent on trying to implement my will on others that I was oblivious to the larger issues involved.

I always wanted to be right. I wanted to be persuasive, to have people view the world the way I did. Eventually, though, as I evolved as a leader, I came to understand that wanting to be right all the time is antithetical to being a leader. That's what dictators do. That's what autocrats do. They draw the line in the sand and chop someone's head off if they cross it. They forever are trying to exert their will on the people they're leading. Effective leaders, though, pick their shots. They send out the message that other people's opinions are important, too, are factored into the equation. They are always sending out the message that they are both flexible and sensitive to other people's wishes.

Nothing causes resentment more than a leader who is constantly dictatorial. No one wants to work for a drill sergeant. No one wants to feel as though they're in basic training. No one wants to feel that their opinions are stupid or that they don't count. And if you constantly do these things you are simply asking for repercussions.

Effective leaders lose a few battles in hopes of winning the war.

KNOW YOUR NON-NEGOTIABLES

At the start of the 1999–2000 season, coming off a disappointing season of the year before, one in which I felt that we had gotten away from our fundamentals as a team, I had a meeting. I felt going into that meeting the same way as I do when I'm taking over a new organization, that in many ways we were starting from scratch, even though I was going into my third season.

I had to, once again, present the vision. I had to stir the passion for it. I had to remind them of the methods. Just as important, I had to stress to my players that we had gotten away from our principles the year before and that that was not going to happen again without repercussions. That if the players didn't think pass before shot, defense before offense, team before individual, they simply were not going to play. Regardless of who they were. Regardless of how much money they made. Regardless of any of it.

I told them these issues were non-negotiable. Other things, like missing shots, getting beat on defense, and making poor decisions; these are basketball issues, part of the game. The others —pass before shot, defense before offense—were non-negotiable issues, as were being on time, having a great work ethic, and being happy in the locker room after a win, even if you didn't play at all.

Those were my five non-negotiable items.

Everything else was negotiable: what time we practice, what we wear on the road, what we have to eat. Many of those things are left up to the players. They decide. They are adults and they should have input into many of the things that affect them on a daily, personal level.

Nor will I force them to adapt to my values on these issues, just because I grew up in a different era than they did.

For example:

Shortly into Phil Jackson's first year coaching the Los Angeles Lakers I read a quote of his that criticized his players' short attention spans, essentially blaming rap music for this. Now he may not have been entirely serious about this, but I thought about how Jackson used to have long sideburns when he played for the Knicks in the early seventies and probably listened to Led Zeppelin, and other music his coaches at the time couldn't stand,

and how so much of this is strictly generational. I'm never going to judge my players on their lifestyle choices, because I remember some of mine when I was younger. I remember bell bottoms and long hair. I remember platform shoes. I remember making a fool of myself by wearing clothes I wouldn't be caught dead in now. I remember all these things, even if there are times I wish I didn't. So I don't ask my players to adapt to my era, just as I didn't want my coaches to make me conform to their era when I was a player. I know these things are all peripheral and come and go with the times.

But the five non-negotiable items are my principles as a coach and I will not sacrifice them.

That doesn't mean I can't try to be innovative in some of the methods I use or realize that you can't deal with the contemporary athlete the way you did a generation ago. I'm always looking for better ways to do things, for ways to improve. You always have to strive to be more creative in your methods.

But your principles are sacrosanct.

KEY CHAPTER POINTS

- **Do the Right Thing** You can make mistakes and be forgiven, but dishonesty lingers in people's memories forever. It's much easier to keep your reputation than rebuild it. Lying makes a problem part of your future; truth makes a problem part of your past.

- **Pick Your Battles** If you are going to square off with people, make sure it's over things that are worth fighting for.

- **Know Your Non-Negotiables** You have to be flexible and adaptive and you have to be able to adjust, but you can't sacrifice your core principles.

ABRAHAM LINCOLN

There can be no argument that the Civil War was the defining moment for the United States. We were a fractured nation, divided primarily over states' rights and slavery. What transpired during those four terrible and bloody years was nothing less than a struggle for the soul of the country. Had the outcome been different or certain concessions been made in order to shorten the war, the face of America would almost certainly be unrecognizable today.

We were on the brink of tearing ourselves apart. And had it not been for the iron will and steely resolve of Abraham Lincoln, we just might have succeeded. For Lincoln, in his time, was a man revered by many and despised by an equal number. He was unbending in his belief that this nation had to be reunited if it hoped to fulfill the vision of its founders.

Of course, achieving such a goal was easier said than done, especially in such turbulent times. There were many intelligent, well-meaning individuals who honestly believed in states' rights. Robert E. Lee, one of our greatest military leaders, was among them. Although the West Point–trained Lee loved his country, when push came to shove he resigned his commission in the Union Army and became the leader of the Army of Virginia.

Lee wasn't unique either. This was an era when the majority of citizens never traveled very far from their homes, much less outside their state. And that's where their loyalty lay, not with some abstract government far away in Washington, D.C.

Equally divisive, yet far more inflammatory, was the issue

of slavery. It wasn't hard to find zealots on both sides of this issue, and it's a tribute to Lincoln's great leadership skills that he never caved in to either side, regardless of how hard they pushed him or how unpopular it made him.

Although Lincoln unshackled the chains of slavery by signing the Emancipation Proclamation, it must be remembered that he also struggled with this issue. In fact, he initially hedged on the subject and it wasn't until well into his presidency that he finally resolved to end the practice.

How was Lincoln able to accomplish this? Given all that was going on at the time, how did he manage to hold things together?

The answers are fairly simple: Lincoln was a flexible leader and a shrewd politician. In the history of our country, there has never been another individual who better combined those vital qualities. The majority of great leaders could only have succeeded during the time in which they lived. Lincoln wasn't one of them. With his strength of character, and with his understanding of how—and when—to compromise, Lincoln belongs to the ages.

What made Lincoln so successful was his willingness to take small steps in order to cover a great distance. He knew the people had to feel they had to come to a decision on their own. In this way, Lincoln was uncommonly shrewd. He gave them just enough to gain their interest, and as their interest increased, he gave them more. That way, people were made to feel that they were in on the process from the beginning.

Lincoln was also a great coalition builder, a man who understood that there was a vast mix of motives in his fellow citizens. Given the tenor of the times, Lincoln had no real choice other than to bring people together in a slow and deliberate way. To try and pound a single solution into them would only have led to dismal failure. Lincoln was far too smart and insightful to go down that path.

Lincoln's constituency included hard-core abolitionists, defenders of slavery, and those who wanted to dodge the issue entirely. It was out of such disparate factions that Lincoln had to forge a body of voters who were willing to join him on his quest to end slavery and preserve the Union.

Dealing with the abolitionists presented a unique problem for Lincoln. Their approach to ending slavery, while well-meaning and well-intentioned, was considered by many of their sympathizers to be too radical and too violent. While Lincoln may have agreed in principle with the abolitionists, he was also aware of the firestorm of controversy they were capable of igniting. So in an effort to keep the peace, Lincoln rejected the high ideals of the abolitionists until key portions of his constituency would accept certain parts of that platform.

Lincoln's true genius lay in his ability to compromise. But he also knew that compromise only goes so far and that if you compromise too much or too often, it only leads to chaos. Lincoln was always willing to listen and it often seemed to take a long time for him to act. But once he did, once he had no doubt about what road to travel, it was then, as the writer G. K. Chesterton said, "the thunderbolt fell from the clear heights of heaven."

In Lincoln, we see the classic traits necessary for great leadership: strength, boldness, character, compassion, ethics, high-minded ideals and principles.

And an unwavering belief in his cause.

Although Lincoln was willing to compromise on certain issues and in certain situations, he was never willing to compromise his love for, or his faith in, the Union and its people. All of its people.

It was this intense faith combined with his almighty will that allowed Lincoln to almost single-handedly preserve our past while giving us our future.

5

ACT DECISIVELY

One of the surprising questions people frequently ask themselves when they have either been promoted or hired for a new position of authority is: Do I really want this job?

Many people think they want to be in charge of a group, but they really don't. They want the perks that come with being the leader. They want the salary. They want the power. They want the big office. They want the status. It's the responsibility they don't want.

In the book *Leadership Secrets of Attila the Hun*, author Wess Roberts's wonderful concept is to examine time-honored leadership principles through the practices of the infamous Attila the Hun, the man who took a collection of disparate tribes, unified them, and became one of the most famous leaders in history. Interestingly, Attila the Hun had many leadership traits that are applicable today. You Have to Want to Be in Charge is one of the first chapters.

"There is little more unsettling to Huns than being under the command of a king or chieftain who shows a lack of commitment to his responsibility as a leader," Roberts writes.

That statement is just as true today.

"A chieftain who fails to accept full decision-making responsibility—or who blames others for his own bad decisions—is weak and lacking in an essential inherent quality of leadership," Roberts writes.

Ditto.

Yes, you need many attributes to lead well. You need methods and skills. You need knowledge and techniques. You need good people working for you and you probably need a little luck along the way, too. But if you aren't willing to accept the responsibility that comes with being in charge, then you ultimately will fail. You have to be willing to make the big decisions. You have to be willing to put both your ideas and yourself on the line.

BECOME AN INTENTIONAL LEADER

There's a process to becoming a leader and it's up to you to not only learn what that process is, but be able to benefit from it.

The first step?

You must study people who have been successful as leaders. Whether you call it modeling or using a mentor or simply following people in your profession you admire, the method is the same. You look at people who have been successful leaders and you study them. What do they do? What do they do right?

How do they treat employees?

How do they conduct themselves in meetings?

What do they do in times of crisis?

How do they reward their staff?

You have to learn from people who are successful. You especially have to recognize those traits that enabled them to be successful.

Conversely, if these leaders have had failures, you must ask yourself, What caused these failures? What were the problems and how can I avoid them? What mistakes did they make? What are the problems to stay away from? If you don't deal with these questions, odds are you will simply repeat the same mistakes, all but programming yourself to fail.

You must find out what both the strengths and the weaknesses were. I've done this everywhere I've ever been. I examined the people who came before me and asked this one basic question: Why did they succeed or why did they fail? And if they did fail, what can I do differently?

This is fundamental when you enter any new leadership situation, but it's surprising how many people don't do this. They start a new job and they enter it as though that job is just beginning, as though the things that happened before have no relevance to them. This is foolish. We have to learn from the people who have made the journey before us, both their successes and their failures.

The second step?

Study their methods. This is an offshoot of modeling, only in more depth. Here you are looking for specific things successful leaders do, to see if you can incorporate them into your own arsenal.

The key is to understand all facets of the job before you can become a leader. You just can't step into a leadership role. This isn't daddy's trust fund. It's not something you inherit. That only happens in fairy tales.

In real life you have to grow into the position of leader. I had to start out at twenty-one in coaching in order to be a head coach at twenty-four. I learned the basics. In the beginning I did all the "gofer" things, paying my dues, learning the business from the ground up. I did this at both the University of Hawaii and Syracuse and I realized there are many successful forms of leadership as I witnessed different coaches in my own profession. Then I had to start as a head coach at Boston University, a hockey school that had virtually no basketball tradition and little interest, a blank canvas on which I had to write my own script.

In retrospect, it was the perfect laboratory for a young coach, a place where I could make my share of mistakes in virtual anonymity. It was there that I began to learn how to run my own program, live with the results of my own decisions, be accountable for the success or failure of other people. It was where

I first began to learn how to be a leader. Even if I didn't know it at the time.

In studying various methods of leadership, you will find that there are many ways to lead.

There is the traditional autocratic way, leader as dictator. Often, these are the people we first think of when we think of leaders, the towering figures of history. They ruled with an iron hand, their authority sacrosanct, unquestioned. Then there is the benign way, leader as everyone's friend. It's the style you see in many people today, this desire to be on equal footing with those you are leading, the leader as buddy. And there is a large middle. In fact, it often seems as if there are as many leadership styles as there are leaders.

Take high-profile coaches, for example. There is the understated John Wooden and Dean Smith way. There is the more vituperative Vince Lombardi–Bill Parcells way. All have been very successful, refuting the theory that there is only one correct leadership style.

In fact, there are many different managing styles, for leadership can be an elusive quality. But there is one common denominator that runs through all coaching styles: Excellence is demanded. Regardless of individual styles, all successful leaders do several things:

- They develop roles, determining who's responsible for what within the organization so that everyone is clear on the chain of command.

- They have good time management.

- They implement daily goals.

- They educate for the future, realizing that this is essential in keeping ahead of the competition.

These common methods are your essentials, regardless of your leadership style. But if the underlying methods are similar, despite different management styles, some of the methods have to change with the times.

It's a little like building a home. Why do your methods change? Knowledge.

I learned long ago that you can't treat everyone the same.

One of the things we do is psychologically test our draft choices. I want to know who has low self-esteem and who has high self-esteem, because it will determine what methods I can use to motivate them. You can push people with high self-esteem harder. Because they feel good about themselves, you can set very high expectations for them and invariably they will meet those expectations. There's nothing they feel they can't accomplish.

Conversely, people with low self-esteem tend to be fragile. They tend to doubt themselves, thus when criticized they have a tendency to deflate, as if the very criticism simply reinforces their own image of themselves.

It's only understandable, then, that you would deal with these two groups of people differently. It's your job as the leader to do as much research as possible, to try and find out as much about the people you're leading as possible.

I can't tell you how many times I've been asked over the course of my career what I said at halftime in a game in which we'd played poorly, then came out and played appreciably better in the second half. The implication is that I gave some fire and brimstone speech in the locker room, threatening my team with the loss of all their worldly possessions if they did not come out and play better.

Usually, nothing could be further from the truth.

Most of the times my reaction is the opposite of what most people would expect: I try to pump up the team when we aren't going well, for their egos are fragile then, their self-esteem low. Then I push them when things are going well, for I know they can handle it emotionally.

IMPLEMENT CRISIS MANAGEMENT

Every leader is eventually going to face a crisis at some point in their career. It's as inevitable as death and taxes.

How do you deal with that crisis?

This important question determines whether the crisis is going to be short-lived or going to mushroom in intensity. Clearly, you want to close the window on the crisis, minimize it. But you must understand that how you handle it will go a long way in determining how the particular crisis gets played out—whether that window closes or actually gets wider. You must be decisive.

All of us, when faced with a crisis, wish it would go away on its own accord, whether we are leaders or not. That's human nature. Our initial fantasy is that if we ignore it will go away, like frost evaporating in the morning sunshine. For leaders, though, that's a losing strategy.

You must face the crisis. You must address it and deal with it, before it can be placed into the past. And you must tell the truth. Again, the more you tell the truth the more you put it into the past. That doesn't mean you have to put it on a billboard. Nor does it mean you have to hit people over the head with it, but you must tell the truth.

Let's say you are the leader of a company where someone has been fudging the books. Now the news has gone public and you have a potential scandal on your hands. What do you do?

The first thing to do is gather your lieutenants together. Everyone must be informed, made aware of the entire situation. This is essential. There can be no secrets, no partial explanations, no spinning of the facts. This is you and your key staff, and within the room you want input from everyone. For that to be meaningful they must have all the facts, too.

Once they're made aware of the situation they must have the opportunity to state their opinions and their insights into the situation. This is important in two ways: At one level, it will give you more insight into the people who are working for you. You will be seeing them in a crisis situation. You will see how they handle things, who is emotional and who is not, who is level-headed and who seems to be all but bouncing off the walls. You will see who are the ones coming up with solutions and who are the ones who don't want to own up to the problem.

If nothing else, this will illustrate to you who your future leaders are. The ones who want to skirt the issue, sweep it under the rug if you will, are not people who one day will be leaders.

The second thing is you need their input, their counsel. Everyone must understand one thing, though: It's all right to differ within the room. In fact, it's good. Within the room you want differences of opinion, people who will articulate their ideas and convictions. These people are your management team and the worst thing they can do is goose-step to you simply because you're the boss. But once you leave the room you must have a shared plan, a shared voice. At some point you are all going to walk out of the room and at that point you all have to be on the same page.

Here's another example from my own experience. At certain times I will discuss various things with my assistant coaches, and we will disagree. I encourage them to disagree, to tell me I'm wrong, to get me to look at a certain issue in a different way. So we will toss ideas and opinions around the room and within that climate everyone is equal.

I tell my assistant coaches all the time: Tell me I'm wrong, tell me there's a different way. As a leader, you cannot be afraid of dissent. You are not always going to be right. Your approach is not always the best one. Your take on a particular situation is not always the most perceptive. You need to rely on the people around you, for their insight, their input. This only makes you better. Strong people only make you stronger and that's never more true than during a crisis.

One of the ways I encourage this is to sometimes make everyone write things down. Let's say we're talking about potential trades. Should we keep player X or try to move him? Should we move player X for player Y? This is the lifeblood of the professional basketball business, the kind of discussions we as a staff are often having. So I will ask everyone to write down their thoughts. This makes them accountable. They can't simply equivocate or nod in agreement when someone else says something. It puts them on the record.

"What would you do?" That's the question I ask them.

Eventually, though, I have to make a decision.

"I may be wrong," I tell them. "You may be right. But this time, anyway, we are going to do it this way."

The message?

I am not telling them that I am right and they are wrong. I'm not telling them that they're stupid or that their opinion is meaningless. I am telling them that they may even be right, but that we have a shared plan and that's now going to be called our plan.

Let's look at another example: In the shortened season in 1999 we had a problem on the court in Washington against the Wizards between Antoine Walker and our veteran point guard Kenny Anderson. Antoine complained that Kenny should run the floor when Antoine had the ball in transition and Kenny answered back that he was the point guard and he should have the ball. It was a messy little spectacle, two teammates sniping at each other in public, one of the things that is taboo on a basketball team. In the locker room or on the practice floor is one thing. These little flare-ups can happen in such a pressurized, competitive environment as the one we work in. But on the court is an embarrassment, to them, to me as the coach, to the organization. It can't be tolerated.

So what did we do?

We had two different strategies—a private one, and a public one.

Privately, we fined both players. We also stressed that if it happened again it would be dealt with more severely. The message to both of them was it didn't matter who started it or who was more to blame. They both had embarrassed the organization, we considered the incident serious, and it would not be tolerated again.

Publicly, we had a more complicated strategy.

Although you have to deal with a crisis publicly, the less you say the better.

So we readily admitted the incident between Antoine and Kenny, said that they both were being fined in what was now a team matter, and then started talking about the future. That was our attempt to get people to stop focusing on the incident itself, an integral part of the process of taking a crisis and quickly minimizing it, immediately starting to put it into the past. The quicker you do this the better off you are.

You must manage the crisis.

And you do that by putting your "spin" on a situation. If you don't, someone else will put their own spin on it. Nature abhors a vacuum: so does a news story. Rest assured that if you're not spinning the story someone else is.

The two rules are: Don't give too much information, and when you do provide information provide your spin.

The quicker you put the crisis behind you and begin moving into the future the better. That's the goal and you can't lose sight of that. The quickest way to have a problem turn into a crisis is not to deal it.

Another thing to remember is you cannot place blame on one person. More importantly, the less you place blame the better chance you have of solving the problem. Placing blame not only causes resentment, it leaves negative feelings that will last long after the crisis goes away. What you have to do is say that we're all to blame, but that the situation will be rectified. You give the reasons why the crisis happened and start talking about the future. By doing this you already are starting to put the incident behind you.

Share the blame and point to the future.

My experience coaching the Knicks taught me that you can't knock your players. It was something I learned from an older assistant named Fuzzy Levane who told me that Red Holtzman, the great Knick coach from the early seventies when the Knicks won two world championships, never knocked his players to the media. If you do publicly knock your players, you are simply creating a crisis. It's one thing to criticize players privately, quite another to do it publicly. When I was coaching the Knicks I quickly learned that I could criticize Patrick Ewing in private. If we were having a private conversation he would accept criticism very well. But Patrick did not like to be criticized in front of his peers. Most people don't.

Criticizing people publicly is also not a good strategy pragmatically.

For instance, let's say I'm unhappy with a particular player and would like to trade him. The worst thing I can do is go to the media and say how unhappy I am with this player and list his deficiencies as if I'm going down a grocery list. All that's going to do is lower that player's value. What I'm trying to do is build assets, not liabilities. At some level it's all about assets and liabilities, not about being right.

So much wasted time is spent on trying to he right. As a young person you want to be right all the time. It's part of your ego. It's part of your competitive nature and often you see it as simply another form of winning.

It's the wrong strategy.

I don't know how much I've grown as a basketball coach in the past ten years, but I know I know more about what *not* to do than I did a decade ago. I'm more battle-tested. I've learned that you have to learn to speak wisely, because you cannot take words back. Once they're said they're a little like newborn babies, they take on a life of their own, and if you've spoken unwisely those words will come back to haunt you.

Examine what happened to John Calipari when he was coaching the New Jersey Nets. Now I've known John since he was a camper at the Five Star basketball camp and I know that he doesn't use ethnic slurs.

But he got into an argument with a reporter after a practice one day. In itself, this was nothing, one of those spontaneous combustion things that can happen. But John got angry and referred to the writer as a "Mexican idiot." That one mistake got him in trouble, turned a run-of-the-mill disagreement that undoubtedly would have been soon forgotten into a nasty little story that made the New York papers—one that John had to publicly apologize for.

These are the things that get young leaders in trouble. The throwaway line that makes you feel better at the moment, the words spoken in times of anger, the attempt at one-upmanship, and trying to always win the argument. At times, we all fall victim to these things. We've all said words we wish we could call back as soon as we uttered them. As a leader, though, the stakes are higher.

That's why I cannot always respond to criticism, even though I may want to.

In the eight years I was the coach at Kentucky I never read the *Lexington Herald-Leader*. When I first arrived in Kentucky I was told the *Herald-Leader* was both critical and out to get the Kentucky basketball program. Both Joe B. Hall, one of the former coaches, and my secretary told me that. True or untrue, I decided simply not to read it. It was out of my life. I had the *Louisville Courier* and *USA Today* delivered to my home every morning, but not the Lexington paper. That way I could deal with the *Herald-Leader* sports writers who covered us in a professional manner. Because I didn't read them, and didn't know what they wrote, when I dealt with them it was never personal.

It can't be personal; nor should it be.

As a leader you are a professional and you must deal with people in a professional way, even the people who may be publicly criticizing you. They have their own job to do, complete with its own demands and pressures, and sometimes their needs and yours are antithetical. That's just the way it is. You can't personalize it. It doesn't mean you have to like it or agree with it. It doesn't mean that you have to send a Christmas card to that person. But you can't personalize it. That's the big mistake people make.

How do I keep from personalizing it?

It's a discipline. Just like being organized and having a great work ethic is a discipline.

Another thing to understand is that if you do personalize things with a member of the media, you are only setting yourself up for even greater problems, for you really can't win. The scenario invariably plays out like this: You respond to the original criticism, then the person who first criticized you responds. The result? The situation escalates, while your main function is to de-escalate the criticism.

What you have to do is handle your criticism strategically, decisively. As a leader, you know you will be criticized, so the question becomes: How do you minimalize it? How do you handle it?

I learned one way of dealing with criticism in New York over a decade ago, when I coached the New York Knicks. My first year there I became friendly with Fred Kerber, one of the sports writers who covered the Knicks. We just hit it off. We talked about our families, we talked about our kids, we talked about all sorts of things. Very little had to do with basketball or the team. We just enjoyed talking to each other.

In retrospect, it was one of the biggest mistakes I made in New York. Why? Because the other writers resented it. They thought I was giving Fred all kinds of insights and observations about the team that I wasn't giving them. They thought I was playing favorites and there was a backlash. The lesson I learned was that I had to be the consummate professional and treat everyone the same way.

In the midst of managing a crisis, or even just managing the day-to-day activity, a mistake a leader can make is getting too concerned about things that don't really matter.

You cannot waste your energy on things that are irrelevant, nor can you waste your energy on things over which you have no control. Nor can you waste your energy on matters that pull you off in different directions, so that you always are bouncing from one brush fire to the next like some frenetic Smokey the Bear. This is a trap many people fall into, whether it's by micromanaging or not having enough faith in your lieutenants.

It's tempting to focus on smaller issues that crop up to postpone thinking about tough decisions, but all of these things take you away from your vision.

They get in the way of decisive action. Being a leader is difficult enough without succumbing to distractions.

DON'T BE AFRAID TO FAIL

On the surface that might sound strange, but it's really not. There are all sorts of people in management positions who don't really want the responsibility that comes with the job. Oh, they want the perks that come with management positions, all right: the money, the power, and the status. They have no trouble with the spoils.

It's the downside of being a leader they don't want.

We see this in sports all the time. There are many very talented basketball players who don't want the ball in crucial situations. They don't want to take the last shot. They don't want the pressure of having the game rest on their shoulders. They are, quite simply, afraid to fail.

And it's not just in sports.

Let's take a look at a typical business meeting:

In a conference room is the CEO and a dozen of his top lieutenants. The CEO has made his position clear on a particular topic and now there is discussion on that topic.

How many people in that room are going to say they agree with the CEO simply because he's the CEO? Odds are, a lot. Let's forget for a second if that CEO's style is to encourage opposition. Many people simply don't want to take the risk of being thought of as wrong. They would rather go along with the flow. They don't want the inherent pressure of disagreeing with the boss, of having their ideas put under a microscope for everyone else to examine. Most don't have the self-assurance, especially if that boss's particular style is to discourage any opposition.

You can't be afraid to be wrong. Let's face it, you are not going to be right all the time; no one is. But acting decisively and with courage are marks of a true leader who people will want to follow.

KEY CHAPTER POINTS

● **Become an Intentional Leader** You must want to be a leader. Set out to learn the methods other successful leaders have used. Study their methods. Learn what worked and what didn't. Be familiar with a variety of leadership styles and find out what works best for you

● **Implement Crisis Management** How you manage a crisis determines whether it escalates or starts to go away. You must face it, deal with it, then put your own spin on it, all in the context of a strategy that includes your entire management team.

● **Don't Be Afraid to Fail** There are all sorts of people who want the perks that come with leadership, but they really don't want the responsibility. In basketball it's the player who doesn't want to take the last shot. In business, it's the person who doesn't want to speak out in the meeting for fear of being wrong. You can't be afraid to be wrong. You can't be afraid to fail.

MARGARET THATCHER

Margaret Thatcher's toughness as a leader is best reflected in the many nicknames bestowed upon her by both admirers and foes. Through the years, Thatcher, a self-admitted "hard nut to crack," has at times been referred to as "the Iron Lady" and "Battling Maggie."

Considered the most outstanding peacetime British prime minister of the twentieth century, Thatcher was the first woman to hold that position. She came to power with the odds for success stacked heavily against her, yet she was elected prime minister three times, another twentieth century first. By the time she left office in 1990, the term *Thatcherism* was an internationally recognized term signifying her particular brand of conservative politics.

Like many great leaders, Thatcher's early life was humble and relatively uneventful. The daughter of a greengrocer, Thatcher was an excellent student, eventually earning a degree in chemistry from Oxford. Several years later, after earning a law degree, she became a successful attorney specializing in tax law.

In 1959, Thatcher, by now married to a business executive and the mother of twin daughters, joined the Conservative Party and was elected to the House of Commons. As minister of Education and Science from 1970 to '74, she provoked a storm of outrage by abolishing free milk in the schools. It was the first glimpse of what lay at the core of Thatcher's beliefs—the less government involvement the better.

Thatcher became head of the Conservative party in 1975.

Four years later, vowing to reverse Britain's woeful economic decline and to reduce the role of government, she was elected as Great Britain's prime minister.

From the very beginning of her tenure, Thatcher was a controversial leader who clashed openly and loudly with her opponents. Even within her party, which was badly divided at the time, there were many voices of dissent. But Thatcher was undeterred and through sheer force of will and personality, she managed to prevail.

To halt Great Britain's downward economic slide, Thatcher proposed agendas and ideas that were radically different from anything previously offered. One of her great strengths as a leader was her willingness to break from the past. She was never afraid to ruffle feathers. It was her strong belief that the British were "living on borrowed time"' unless sweeping economic and societal changes were implemented. Naturally, many Brits, including some within her own party, viewed such notions with great skepticism.

In 1982, Thatcher proved herself to be tough-minded and decisive in military matters. When Argentine forces occupied the Falkland Islands, Thatcher quickly sent in a task force and quelled the Argentines and reclaimed the islands for Great Britain. Her performance during the Falkland crisis earned her high praise, even from her opponents.

At the heart of Thatcher's political philosophy was the strong desire to decrease the role of government in the economy. To achieve her goal, she privatized many national industries and social programs, including education, housing, and health care. She also worked hard to curb the power of trade unions.

Thatcher's brand of conservatism had much in common with that of Ronald Reagan. Reaganomics and Thatcherism were philosophical soul mates that stressed private enterprise over government intervention. Also, their shared belief that a strong national defense is the best offense played a critical role in bringing about sweeping changes in the once-powerful Soviet Union.

Thatcher always had a strong moral sense of right and wrong. She always believed in simple truths and constantly searched for first principles. She felt that the true purpose of government was to present people with ideas and opportunities.

However, Thatcher didn't earn her nicknames by being particularly easy to deal with. On the contrary, she could be unbending and impossible to persuade. Her tendency to micromanage, and her blunt argumentativeness, gave fuel to her many critics. Although she loved to argue her case, and to invite the opinions of others, she was always determined that her view would win out in the end. She could be especially tough on those with opposing views, often to the point of cutting them off in midsentence.

Thatcher once said of her leadership style: "I never tried to get consensus. I tried to get agreement with what I wanted to do."

Margaret Thatcher came to office promising to reduce inflation, denationalize basic industries, and limit the power of trade unions. It was a sweeping and controversial agenda, one that wasn't embraced with great eagerness by the staid, tradition-bound British. And although Thatcher, and Thatcherism, didn't succeed on all fronts, it cannot be denied that many British people were much better off when she retired in 1990 than when she became prime minister eleven years earlier.

By changing the landscape of politics in Great Britain, Margaret Thatcher distinguished herself as one of the strongest, most influential leaders of this century.

6

BE ADAPTABLE

The morning after we won the national championship in 1996 at Kentucky, we had a staff meeting. We had been up all night celebrating. We had reveled in the moment, the incredible feeling of realizing that you are at the very top of the mountain, that all the hard work and all the preparation and all the sacrifice had brought us to this one unbelievable moment, this time that we all would remember for the rest of our lives.

My goal that morning was to get back to that moment. The question was: How? I wanted their ideas.

One person suggested that we had to have a great recruiting class.

"How long will that take before we see the results of that payoff?" I asked.

"Two or three years," he said.

"Do you want to wait that long?" I asked.

We talked about it for a while and eventually I told everyone to go off on vacation and come back in ten days and tell me how we could get back to the Final Four. Ten days later they did. They literally came back with pages of ideas on how to do it.

My message to them was we had to start outsmarting everybody. They heard me and they executed it.

We started the next season very well, with getting back to

the Final Four as our goal. Then, midway through the season, Derek Anderson—one of our two stars—went down for the year with a serious knee injury. It was a devastating loss, one that at least on the surface could have realistically finished any hopes of getting back to the Final Four.

So what did we do? We had another meeting.

"How do we overcome this?" I asked my staff.

Once again I was looking for creative ideas. How could we continue to win without Derek Anderson? What adjustments could we make? What could we do differently?

We came up with some other ideas of how to play better and we worked on them. Eventually, we continued to win and did indeed achieve our goal and got back to the Final Four, where we lost to Arizona in the national championship game.

And the lesson we all learned? You have to keep changing things. You have to be more creative.

Let's examine the Ron Mercer trade that we did in the summer of 1999.

When I first came to the Celtics in 1997 my plan was to rebuild the team through the draft. It was a plan based on the realities of the NBA at the time, as I perceived them to be. At the time, the highest-paid salary in the league was about $11 million a year. But that summer Kevin Garnett, the great young player for the Minnesota Timberwolves, was given a contract for roughly $120 million, one that instantly changed the financial landscape of the league.

My reality with the Celtics is that I'm given a budget by owner Paul Gaston. Given the new economic situation of the NBA, my original plan will not work, for the simple reason that under our budget we simply do not have enough money to pay all our young talented players what they want. Since we had given Antoine Walker roughly $70 million in the summer of 1998, when it came time the following summer to deal with Ron Mercer—who had one year remaining on his original contract—I knew that we could not re-sign him. He simply was going to want more money than we had to pay him. The fact that he had played for me at Kentucky was not enough to keep him in Boston. The fact that he had begun his professional career with the Celtics was not enough. As a professional athlete with a short window to make the big money, Ron had decided it was in his best interest to go somewhere else that, in theory anyway, could pay him the kind of money he was seeking.

Did I want to trade Ron Mercer? No. He has the potential to be one of the top off-guards in the league.

But that's the economic reality of the game. It's pointless, therefore, to begrudge Ron Mercer, as it's pointless to simply throw up your hands and moan about the contemporary athlete. That's just beating a dead horse.

You simply must adjust and move on.

Once we had decided that Ron was unsignable, our strategy then became to get as much as we could for him. It was not to try to convince Paul Gaston that he had to come up with more money for Ron Mercer, nor was it to complain about our fate. Our strategy was to adapt and try to turn the situation into a positive one.

What we did was trade Ron to Denver for Danny Fortson, Eric Williams, Eric Washington, and a future first-round draft pick. We also unloaded Dwayne Schintzius, who had been a gamble the year before and who hadn't worked out, and Popeye Jones, whose career had been slowed down by injuries. By trading Ron that also allowed us to sign Calbert Cheaney as a free agent, a player who plays the same position as Ron does, and also open up a roster slot for Adrian Griffin that we got when we released Eric Washington.

The theory was that Fortson, a tough inside rebounder who had been one of the best in the league in rebounding the year before, and Williams—who had spent his first two years in the league with the Celtics—would give us a more physical presence underneath. All this and a future first-round draft choice, too.

Was it a good trade?

Like all trades, the future will decide. What you try to do when you can't sign an athelete is try to get fifty cents—seventy cents—on the dollar. Get as much as you can, and move on.

The point is that we took the inevitable loss of Ron Mercer and did something to try to make out team better, not just sit around and bemoan our fate.

Your job as a leader is to find ways to win, not look for excuses for why you lose.

That's what adaptability is all about.

One postscript to this story: During one of our staff meetings before the trade, my assistant coach Jim O'Brien said, "Rick, you simply have to go see Paul Gaston and convince him that he has to give Ron the money."

"That's not where we're going to spend our energy," I told Jim. "We are going to live within the budget he's given us and find a way to make it work."

Afterward, though, I took Jim with me to go visit Paul Gaston.

Was it to try to convince Paul that he needed to spend more money?

No.

I wanted Jim O'Brien to learn what I already knew. Paul told him that, unlike some of the other teams in the NBA, the Celtics were a family business; that he wasn't in it for the ego or the recognition. He was in the professional basketball business to make money. Paul also told him his philosophy about the NBA's salary cap: how it was established as a way for the NBA owners to police themselves, but from the beginning everyone has been trying to find more and more creative ways to circumvent it and he is simply not going to do that.

That is Paul Gaston's philosophy and I have to find ways to succeed within that system. Did Paul Gaston mislead me when he hired me? No.

Would I like to have the resources like the Knicks and the Lakers have? Sure. But I don't. And that's not anything revelatory. In essence, Gaston's philosophy of working within the salary cap is what makes the NFL the most competitive sport, so I can't complain about his philosophy. In virtually every department in every business there is a CEO who is going to tell you you can't have this or you can't have that. There's always going to be some kind of restraint on you, fiscal or otherwise. It's your job as a leader to adapt and create opportunity where limits exist.

You can't overdramatize your situation, like so many people do. You can't stand in awe of the supposed enormity of the task ahead. You can't simply say that you didn't realize the obstacles that were going to be placed in your path. You have to face it, attack it, solve it, and move on.

Leaders can't complain. They must keep adapting.

STAY CREATIVE

Let's look at the NBA as an example: Salaries have changed, players have changed, the media has changed, and marketing has changed. Everything has changed. It's a microcosm of society.

Change is part of the natural order of things and you must change with it or get left behind. How quickly can you adapt? How quickly can you rebuild? These are the questions.

We live in a "quick-fix" society. There's no getting around that. People may say they know a company must rebuild and that this is a process that's going to take some time. They may even believe it philosophically. But all too few have the patience for it. They want to see results right away. If they don't see them, they will start to have doubt.

You see this with sports teams all the time. Some coach gets fired, the franchise is in the depths. A new coach is hired. He comes in and starts talking about how he is going to rebuild and it's going to take a few years, but eventually the rewards will be worth the wait. And everyone nods his head in agreement. Then shortly into the next season—if things aren't appreciably better—everyone wants to know what's the matter.

An oversimplification? Not really.

This is an example of the sense of urgency we talked about in the first chapter. It's not a perfect world. You don't have unlimited time. People are not going to give you all sorts of leeway simply because you've been successful in the past or that they like your vision. The clock is always ticking. The old adage is true, even if it's cruel: It's not what you've done; it's what have you done for me lately?

The key is you have be creative, keep looking for new and innovative ways to do things. One of the things I did at Kentucky, which was controversial at the time, was to have denim uniforms. There were many in the state who thought that sacrilegious, an affront to the Kentucky tradition. I disagreed, arguing that the great tradition of Kentucky basketball was certainly a lot more than the texture of the uniforms. Besides, it was a business decision. I was looking for ways to increase revenue and there weren't many. Rupp Arena was sold out. Our television package was maxed out. Our traditional revenue sources had capped out. About the only thing left was marketing. The uniform change dramatically increased marketing.

Another thing I did at Kentucky, which was controversial at the time, was to hire Bernadette Locke as an assistant coach, making her the first woman in the country to be an assistant coach in a men's program in college basketball.

Was hiring her a marketing strategy?

Yes, it was.

If I had hired a man it would have made the transactions section of the sports page. By hiring a woman, who had been an ex-collegiate standout as a player, someone who was going to have an important role in recruiting and handling job placement for our players after graduation, this was news. Bernadette was on the cover of four different magazines. This publicity was a godsend for a scandal-ridden program. But Bernadette was also an outstanding assistant coach and helped us get a great recruiting class. She made a difference. She gave us an edge.

Then again, everywhere I've coached I felt I needed a gimmick, a certain edge. At Boston University it was the full-court press. At Providence College it was both the full-court press and the frequent use of the three-point shot. At another level, though, it had to give us an edge and I thought that Bernadette would be very good in recruiting, would make us different.

Not that it's easy to keep adapting.

When we are young we are more willing to try new things, experiment with new ideas. It's a time in life when we are searching to find our way in the world, trying out different roles. That is one of the strengths of youth, the ability to look at change with fresh eyes.

The older we get the more we have a tendency to become set in our ways. We have arrived at a certain comfort zone. We like our steak cooked a certain way. We like a certain kind of music, a certain car. We dress a certain way, drive to work a certain way. We have developed certain habits over a period of time that are very comfortable to us, familiar. We know what we like and what we don't like. Change is disruptive. It challenges people's belief systems, is disorienting. Change becomes the enemy.

You must fight through this.

You must keep growing, adding to your arsenal. You can't be content to rest on your past accomplishments, but rather must keep pushing your personal envelope. Like Michael Jordan, who added a fallaway jumper to his offensive repertoire in the latter years of his career, a time when his wondrous athleticism was starting to slip just a little. Did Jordan need the fallaway jumper to remain great? No. Michael Jordan was still going to be great regardless. But adding that shot allowed him to continue to be unstoppable at a time in his career when age had started to be a factor.

Not only must you be flexible, but so must the people you are leading.

This is crucial in today's highly competitive world where the technology is exploding all around us and companies are downloading and streamlining. In this climate people can't afford not to change. They can't say they're too old or too set in their ways. They can't keep clinging to the past, simply because it was more comfortable or because "that's the way we always did it." These excuses no longer are viable. It's really very simple: They either change or they're going to get left behind, like people on the sidewalk staring after some long-gone parade.

So you have to keep changing.

And the people around you must keep changing, too. They really don't have a choice. Not if they want to stay viable in today's world.

ADOPT FLEXIBLE PROBLEM SOLVING

I am not only the coach of the Boston Celtics, I am also the president, thus my concerns are not just how many games we win. I'm also concerned with how we market our product, how appealing it is to our fans, how the Boston Celtics are perceived in the community. And if it's certainly true that winning solves a lot of ills, I always have to be thinking of the big picture and not simply the next game.

For instance, after every game I meet with the media. This usually takes place about ten minutes afterward and is not always an easy thing to do. As a coach, you are still wrapped up in the emotion of the game, still decompressing. Often, the last thing you want to do is talk to the media, especially after a tough loss. What you really want to do is go off somewhere by yourself and lick your wounds. You can't. Dealing with the media is part of the job and something I have learned to do over the years, even in those times when I don't really want to. And in all these sessions I am speaking to the fans, too, not just the media, and my message must be geared to the future. This is especially true in times of adversity.

The routine is always the same. After a game I go into the locker room and spend a few minutes with the team. If we won,

I tell them why. If we lost, I do the same thing. Either way, I look for reasons why the game played the way it did. The plan is to reinforce good things and use failures as learning tools.

Let's say, for example, that we've just lost a game.

I tell the players why we lost, the specific things we did not do, the reasons we are all feeling so badly right now. This is imperative. Everyone knows we lost. The important thing is to know why, so we can instantly start to use the loss as a learning experience. I do the same things after a win, but after a loss it's crucial. Without being able to use it as a learning vehicle, a loss is just a loss.

Then I go into my office for a few minutes and compose myself, think about what I'm going to say to the media when I meet with them in a few minutes. I jot down some notes. These are not only about the actual game, but about the Celtics. Especially if we have lost. I look over the statistical information from the game, look at the schedule, start thinking about the future.

I must not only answer questions about why we lost, but I have to try to put a positive spin on it, for the good of the organization. I cannot go into the media room, say we stunk, and walk out, even though as the coach I might want to do that. I try to be upbeat, a little glib. That was something I had to teach myself to do and it didn't come easily. In the beginning trying to be upbeat and glib after a loss was foreign to me.

But leaders can't hide from adversity. They must be visible.

As the president of the organization, however, I want our fans to believe in our vision of the future, too; that, yes, things might be difficult now, but there is a plan and it's going to eventually work. That's our vision and it must always be reinforced, even when we're struggling. I can never lose sight of that. So I am always selling the Celtics, not just explaining why we lost a particular game.

That's not to say our fans shouldn't get upset when we don't play well. They are paying good money, they have high expectations, and when we don't measure up to the standards they have for us they're not happy. That's understandable. They want a good performance. But I'd rather have them come to the Fleet-Center and boo and encourage the team, not discourage it.

As long as there's hope for the future your marketing will not suffer. Fans can live with a team that's struggling as long as they believe in the future. It's a little like buying a stock. Most people will ride out the tough times as long as they believe that eventually they will make money on that stock. And in a sense, fans *are* the stockholders in your company. So I must always be thinking of them and try to be cognizant of what they're thinking. Every press conference I give I'm conscious of what I say from a marketing standpoint.

You have to recognize problems right away.

These problems in your organization might not necessarily be bad people, but they are people who don't share your philosophy. My first year with the Celtics we had three of them: Dee Brown, Eric Williams, and Travis Knight.

Dee Brown was simply a veteran who I felt wasn't flexible enough to buy into what we were trying to do.

Eric Williams was a time-management problem. He was a young player who had a reputation for often not being on time and also had come to camp the year before having gained considerable weight in the off-season. When I got to the Celtics one of my first plans was to get everyone into a serious off-season conditioning program. Sean Brown, our strength coach, flew to Eric's home town of Newark, New Jersey, to set up his program for him. Eric didn't show up. Sean rescheduled, once again flew to New Jersey. Again, Eric failed to show. This time I called Eric's agent and said that the next time Eric missed an appointment I was going to trade him.

That's what happened. He missed another appointment and I quickly traded him to Denver. These are the things you simply don't need in an organization.

More times, though, your success depends on your ability to

solve problems. We also do this with our own players. Take Antoine Walker, for example.

In the 1999 season he was having a problem with shot selection. When he took good shots he shot a decent percentage. When he took more difficult shots, his percentage declined. Yet when I pointed this out to him he would immediately get defensive. He would invariably see that as criticism.

So one of the things we did for Antoine was make a computer printout of every shot he took. Then we broke it down for him. We showed him that he shot 34 percent from the three-point line, 27 percent from the three-point line to fifteen feet, 50 percent in the low post.

How did he react to this? He liked it. It had given him another medium. This wasn't some coach getting on him about taking bad shots. He could see it right there in black and white, could see the statistics. We give him all the statistical information, so he can make up his own mind what's a good shot for him and what is not. I don't have to tell him, he can see for himself. And you know that he is going to like anything that gives him the opportunity to score points.

That's problem solving.

We also did the same thing with Grant Hill, one of the best young players in the league, an emerging superstar with the Detroit Pistons. Then we showed Antoine the printout we did on Grant Hill. Why is Hill playing better? Because he's taking higher percentage shots. Again, I don't have to tell Antoine this; it's something he sees for himself. It is a way to give Antoine a lesson without having to hit him over the head with it.

And this approach relates very well to any business. You use the statistics, the hard data, to try to convince employees to change their behavior. You have the technology. Use it.

Let's say, for example, that you think your young salesman is getting off track and that his production is suffering because of it. Yet if you tell him you think he's in a slump his first response invariably will be that it's not him, it's the product. His initial response will be defensive. You're either picking on him or else misreading the situation. Either way, you are singling him out. He will look for someone else to blame instead of looking at himself. That's human nature and you as the leader must understand that.

So, if possible, let the data say it for you.

Understand that young people are different and it's not simply because they're younger. They don't want "fatherly advice." They don't like to be told what they're doing wrong. Do it often enough and they eventually will tune you out. Young people are also growing up with computers and technology. This is what they relate to, what they understand, how they have come to perceive the world. Young people have to "see it." In many ways they respond more to this than they do to people talking to them. So let the technology show them what they're doing wrong. Let the technology show them how they can be better.

They've come of age in an increasingly visual society, products of the new on-screen technology. This is the way they perceive the world. They have grown up with computers and video games that didn't exist a generation ago. My kids, for example, are on the computer every night. They're online. They're in chat rooms. They use E-mail. This is what young people relate to, what they're comfortable with. They want factual information. They want to see it, not hear it, so use this.

That's problem solving, too.

Another example:

In the 1999 season Paul Pierce was a rookie for us. He had been a great player at Kansas, only to inexplicably slip to tenth in the 1998 draft, where we were very fortunate enough to be able to draft him. From the beginning it was apparent he was one of the elite rookies in the league, a star in the making.

It also was apparent that when he was playing well he exuded confidence. If he wasn't playing well, he seemed to deflate right in front of you. His entire body language was different, to the point that he became a different player.

It was mind-boggling to me. But do I try to figure this out?

No, I don't.

If I did, odds are his initial response was to say that I'm wrong, he doesn't do that. He will immediately get defensive. He will think I am being critical of him and he will not like that. But if I can show it to him he can see it himself.

So I showed him. We videotaped him and let him see it himself.

Young people have to "see it." And you have to do everything you can to enable them to.

That's problem solving, too.

We are always showing players videotape of themselves and the people they play against. The more examples we show them the better.

ADAPT TO CHANGES

How do you know when to make changes?

Let's set up a situation:

You have a negative, cynical person whose presence is poisoning the entire fabric of your organization, even though this person is productive.

What do you do?

The first thing you do is address the situation. This is essential. The worst thing you can do is 1) ignore it, and hope it get gets better on its own, or 2) rationalize that because this person does produce you can live with his attitude. This kind of attitude cannot be tolerated. These kind of people are problems and if they're not going to change they must be removed. If they're not, they will only drag down the entire organization. There's no underestimating this.

So you deal with this person one-on-one. You call them in

and explain the problem you're having with them. The first thing that will happen when you begin to question this person's attitude is they will deny it. They will immediately get defensive and start to make excuses for their behavior. They will point out that they are producing more than other people are so why aren't we focusing on those people who are not producing?

You tell them that their behavior is hurting the organization, that their cynicism, their negativity, is deflating the people around them and that they must change. They have no choice.

DON'T BE CONFRONTATIONAL

This shouldn't be said in an aggressive, confrontational manner. Quite the opposite. The message should be forceful, but the manner low key. You are telling this employee that this is essentially non-negotiable, that you are not looking for a philosophical debate. This is the way the organization is going to run and the employee has to decide whether he wants to be a part of it or not. And it's not multiple choice. There's only one correct answer.

So it's really up to the employee.

He has been told that there's a problem and now he must decide if he's going to do something about it. The scenario's been set. You must wait to see how it plays out.

If the behavior doesn't improve, you bring him in again.

Only this time you tell him that if he can't change, that if he can't adapt to the style of the organization, then maybe it's better that he leaves. You tell him that it's not a matter of who is right and who is wrong, simply that his behavior is not fitting into the organization and it probably will be better for everyone if he moves on. Again, the key is not to do anything that's going to turn this into a debate. The message is that there is no longer a choice. He was told there was a problem; he essentially has done little to correct it. Now it's best for everyone that there's a change.

This is one of the toughest things that you will have to do.

Letting people go is not pleasant, especially people who are producing. But you must understand that, invariably, there will be a significant number of people who won't change. At least not initially. To many people change is threatening and disruptive and they will quickly revert back to what is comfortable and familiar.

But leadership is all about change. The ones who make it will be the ones who can adapt, who can make things better, all within the context of a critical environment.

That's another thing you must understand: Everyone is a critic today. It's part and parcel of the times we live in and you must not only understand that, but also be able to deal with it. Critics are everywhere, daily snipers.

I learned to insulate myself from criticism many years ago. Sports has changed in the past decade or so, with the profusion of sports talk shows on radio. These shows live off controversy and opinion. If one host says black, the other says white. One says good, the other says bad. All to fuel the constant stream of callers, what I jokingly call the Fellowship of the Miserable.

My way of dealing with it is not to deal with it. I don't listen. Nor do I want the people around me to tell me what's being said.

I will, however, look at the daily stacks of scores and stats, at the daily stack of clippings the organization compiles every day from various newspapers. The only reason I do this is to gauge how the players are responding publicly. Are they down? How are they handling adversity? What's their mood? These questions are of great interest to me, as they not only give me further insight into the state of my team, but if a player is questioning publicly what the coaches are doing this has to be instantly addressed.

A leader's authority cannot be questioned.

The biggest mistake a leader can make is to allow problems to fester. These problems do not just disappear like frost in the noontime sun. They percolate. They boil. They have the potential to grow and spread like weeds. More importantly, they never go away. So you must localize the problem as soon as possible. Your mission is to eradicate the problem, in order to put it behind you as soon as possible.

Whenever anyone questions my authority we go one-on-one. We meet face-to-face. We deal with it. As a leader you cannot let these things slide.

I remember my first exhibition game when I was working as Hubie Brown's assistant coach with the New York Knicks. It was halftime and Hubie got into a disagreement with Truck Robinson, one of the veteran Knicks players.

It began with Hubie telling Truck he wasn't boxing out, that Truck's man had four offensive rebounds.

"I am too boxing out," Truck replied.

"If you're boxing out then why does your man have four offensive rebounds?" Hubie asked.

"If you think it's so easy boxing him out, Hubie, why don't you do it?" Truck said.

I couldn't believe it. I had been around basketball all my life, mostly college, and I had never seen this kind of insubordination from a player before.

Hubie and Truck continued to go back and forth, the exchange escalating, before Hubie told Truck he was going to fine him a thousand dollars.

At the end of the halftime, shell-shocked, I walked out of the locker room.

"Hey, kid," Hubie said to me. "What did you learn from that exchange?"

I wasn't sure how to respond. My first thought was never anger a player like that in public. I eventually told Hubie I didn't know.

"Always get the last word in with these guys," Hubie said.

That was my NBA baptism, but I have laughed at this story for many years. That's NBA basketball. My message in these situations is that we are all part of the same team. That we are, in a certain sense, in a partnership, one in which we all will benefit if the organization is successful. We all must be on the same page. That doesn't mean we can't have differences or varying opinions. It doesn't mean that everyone has to be some robot, marching to some party line. That doesn't mean that behind closed doors people can't tell me that they think I'm wrong. But we all must embrace the same overall vision; all must realize that we, indeed, are in a partnership.

It's one of the first things I say in my initial meeting with the team. I tell them that their job when talking to the media is to protect their family—and in this case their family is the team. I also ask them one simple question when they go public with their discontent:

"What are you gaining?"

For instance, let's say a player leaves the Celtics and immediately voices his displeasure, whether it's about me, the other coaches, the organization, the city, or whatever. What good does that do him, other than venting? In fact, it appreciably hurts him.

In a pragmatic sense it hurts him because the word gets around that he's acted this way. Sports, like business, is in many ways an insular world, one in which people are connected, an extended fraternity if you will. Word gets out that this player is a disloyal malcontent, someone who goes public with his displeasure. Rest assured, no player wants this on his résumé. This kind of baggage always has the potential to hurt him down the road, for in any business you never know what the future is going to bring, nor the people with whom you one day might be working.

Eric Williams is a perfect example:

One of the first things I did when I got the Celtics job was move Eric Williams, basically because I didn't like his work ethic and the fact that he was often late. I saw him as a potential problem and I simply wasn't going to tolerate that. So he was traded to Denver for two second-round draft choices.

Two years later, in the summer of 1999, he came back to the Celtics in the Ron Mercer trade. Why did I take him back? Two reasons. Eric Williams never went public with his displeasure when he was traded the first time. And he admitted that that trade had been a sort of wakeup call and that he had rededicated himself to his career. So when he came back he came back as a mature player who acted like a professional.

A player must act like a professional, too, when he leaves an organization. He should thank the organization for the opportunity and move on. When he reacts negatively it almost always reflects badly on him, for people think twice about hiring people who cannot control their emotions. Again, the key is to be a professional. Don't personalize it, even if that may feel better in the short term. This is business. It must be handled as such.

* * *

There also are other ways to get your message across to someone you are leading rather than confronting them from across a desk.

For example:

Let's say that I know that one of my players is discontented. I find a way to talk to him in a neutral environment, like maybe an adjoining seat on a plane. Or I may simply go up to him casually after practice.

Here's how it might play out.

"I can tell something's bothering you," I say.

"Why do you say that?" the player says.

"Because you're just not yourself," I say. "You're not the same. What's going on?"

The key here is this is not a confrontational situation, like dealing with someone in your office has the potential to be. This style is low-key, nonthreatening, is in a different, "safer" environment. The atmosphere is of two colleagues, not of boss/employee.

It also allows that person to see you in a different light. Maybe it allows that person to see that you have a sense of humor, that everything isn't always deadly serious. The old adage really is true—humor really can be the best medicine.

The point is you can't be the boss every minute.

Yes, you're the decision maker. But you're not the absolute ruler. You can't be. It's a totally different environment than it used to be. A different society. A different culture. Virtually a different country. Certainly it's different than when I was a player at the University of Massachusetts in the early seventies. Back then coaches were absolute dictators. Leaders also were absolute dictators. Their authority was unquestioned, their words all but etched in stone.

I first saw this begin to change over a decade ago, back when I was an assistant coach with the New York Knicks. Hubie Brown was the coach and he was almost the archetype of the old-time coach. He was authoritarian, with a dominating presence, almost as if delivered from Central Casting, and it was inconceivable to me that any of the players would ever talk back to him or question his authority. But they did. Not all of them, certainly. Not all the time, of course. But it was soon apparent that there were chips in the old order and it was starting to crumble.

You must not only understand this, but be able to deal with it, too.

For two things happen to leaders who don't adapt:

1) They get paranoid and adopt the belief that everyone is out to get them.

2) They get left behind, for the simple reason that their competition is always adapting.

KEY CHAPTER POINTS

● **Stay Creative** It does you no good to dwell on excuses for why
you are not being successful, even if they're correct. That's simply self-defeating. Your job as a leader is to find ways to be im-
proving, find ways to win, not to look for excuses for why you
lose. Leaders can't stay stuck. They must adapt.

● **Adopt Flexible Problem Solving** Change is part of the natural order of things, and you must either change with the times or
be left behind. How quickly can you adjust? How quickly can you
adapt? How quickly can you rebuild? These are key questions.
And you must understand that you don't have unlimited time. The
clock is always ticking. You have to keep being creative, keep
looking for new and innovative ways to do things. You always
have to keep adding to your arsenal.

● **Adapt to Changes** The biggest mistake a leader can make is
to allow problems to fester. Problems that are not dealt with have
the potential to grow. More importantly, they never go away. So
your goal is to recognize problems right away, deal with them,
and put them behind you as quickly as possible.

● **Don't Be Confrontational** Your message to people who are
complaining, and who are not acting like you want them to act, is
that you are all in a partnership; that you are part of the same
team; and that everyone benefits from the organization being
successful. That doesn't mean you can't have differences, but
what you always must be striving for is for everyone to share the
same vision, and be working to see that vision actualized.

NELSON MANDELA

On the list of the most important human rights victories of our times, the end of apartheid in South Africa has to be near the top. And as often happens with successful movements, a charismatic leader inspired the masses and grew to be a symbol of that victory. The American Revolution had George Washington, the Solidarity movement had Lech Walesa, but there is probably no greater testament to the power of great leadership than the story of Nelson Mandela, a revolutionary who toppled a government from behind bars.

Mandela was raised in the countryside and taught from an early age to have great pride in his people, the Thembu. When he ran away from home as a young man, to escape an arranged marriage, Mandela landed in Johannesburg where he quickly became outraged at the treatment of his fellow blacks under the white minority government.

He first became involved in political organizing against apartheid as a college student, but it was after he set up his own law firm that he became truly dedicated to the cause. Mandela and his law partner Oliver Tambo saw people jailed simply for being unemployed, for living in the wrong area, and other so-called offenses. As Tambo described it, "South African apartheid laws turn innumerable innocent people into 'criminals.' Apartheid stirs hatred and frustration among people. Young people, who should be in school or learning a trade, roam the streets, join gangs, and wreak their revenge on the society that confronts them with only the dead-end alley of crime or poverty."

Changing these conditions became Mandela's mission. But it wasn't long before Mandela and his involvement with the African National Congress—the political party bent on over-throwing apartheid—began to attract the attention of the white South African government, who knew a threat to their stability when they saw one.

First, the authorities demanded that Mandela and Tambo move their practice from the city to the "back of beyond," as Mandela later put it in his autobiography *Long Walk to Freedom*, "miles away from where clients could reach us during working hours. This was tantamount to asking us to abandon our legal practice, to give up the legal service of our people. . . . No attorney worth his salt would easily agree to do that."

Mandela and Tambo were determined to defy the order.

Whenever an obstacle was thrown in Mandela's way, he immediately set upon finding a way around it. Time and time again, Mandela was to be thwarted in his struggle. But instead of throwing up his hands, he would roll up his sleeves and fig-ure out how he could succeed within the conditions at hand—no matter how brutal or unfair they might have been.

In 1952 the heat was on, so Mandela recognized he had to spread his anti-apartheid message—and fast. The authorities were closing in and preventing every standard means of organiz-ing a political movement—using ever crueler variations on the system they had used to oppress the country's black majority for decades.

So Mandela came up with what became known as the M-Plan, named for its creator. Tambo described it as "a simple commonsense plan for organization on a street basis, so that Congress volunteers would be in daily touch with the people, alert to their needs and able to mobilize them. [Mandela could] no longer appear on the public platform and few platforms were allowed us as the years went by, but he was ever among the people, guiding his lieutenants to organize them."

Mandela was putting to work leadership principals he had learned as a boy being raised by his uncle, the powerful acting regent of the Thembu people.

In his autobiography, Mandela recalled attending meetings over which his uncle presided:

"As a leader, I have always followed the principles I first saw demonstrated by the regent at the Great Place. I have always endeavored to listen to what each and every person in a discussion had to say before venturing my own opinion. Oftentimes, my own opinion will simply represent a consensus of what I heard in the discussion.

"I always remember the regent's axiom: 'A leader,' he said, 'is like a shepherd. He stays behind the flock, letting the most nimble go out ahead, whereupon the others follow, not realizing that all along they are being directed from behind.'"

It wasn't long before Mandela was jailed and truly had to completely rely on the more nimble members of his flock. And as always, Mandela adapted and the movement thrived. He was in and out of jail throughout the late fifties and early sixties, sometimes simultaneously representing his clients while conducting his own defense in another courtroom. As the price on his head grew higher, he donned disguises to move throughout the country, earning him the nickname, the Black Pimpernel. He also utilized a complex underground network of people willing to smuggle him out of the country to attend diplomatic meetings where he exhorted other countries to join his fight.

Finally, the South African government caught up with Mandela and handed him a life sentence in 1962. His statement at the trial became a rallying point for the movement during the twenty-seven years he was imprisoned:

"During my lifetime I have dedicated myself to the struggle of the African people. I have fought against white domination and I have fought against black domination. I have cherished the ideal of a democratic and free society in which all persons live together in harmony and with equal opportunities. It is an ideal which I hope to live for and to achieve. But, if needs be, it is an ideal for which I am prepared to die."

And he stuck to his word. Twice the government offered Mandela freedom if he would renounce his ideals. Both times, he firmly refused and his legend grew. "Prisoners cannot enter into contracts," he said. "Only free men can negotiate."

Though Mandela was denied access to the freedom movement he helped ignite, behind the prison walls he once again displayed his irrepressible knack for organizing to better his community and making the best of a very bad situation.

Mandela started a school at the harsh penal island where he served the first part of his sentence. As the prisoners did their grueling manual labor, they quizzed one another on the week's lessons. They even put on plays.

"Any man or institution that tries to rob me of my dignity will lose," Mandela later wrote in a note smuggled out by friends.

In 1990, the white minority government did just that. Bowing to international pressure, President F. W. deKlerk summoned Mandela to the presidential palace to negotiate his own release—and an end to apartheid.

Mandela became president of South Africa in 1991 in the country's first democratic election. On a continent rife with warring factions and political turmoil, Mandela steered his nation through a remarkably peaceful transition to democracy. He simply used the same integrity, openness, and ingenuity that allowed him to prevail over the oppression and imprisonment he encountered on the way to freeing his people. Mandela humbly explains away his remarkable impact on his nation and the world: "I was not a messiah but an ordinary man who had become a leader because of extraordinary circumstances."

7

BE CONSISTENT

How can you be consistent and adaptable, too? Isn't this a contradiction? No. While you must be adaptable with your methods, you also must be consistent with your message.

But it's more difficult to be a leader than ever before.

Once upon a time authority went virtually unquestioned. Parents, teachers, coaches, bosses: they were given the utmost respect because of their title. They said, "Jump!" and people asked, "How high?"

Those days are as far removed as record players and black-and-white television sets. People don't follow blindly anymore. They don't bow down to titles. Many times it's just the opposite. Often, their first response is to question any kind of authority, if not outright rebel against it. They want to know why they're being asked to do things. They want to know what's in it for them. Leaders must understand that they're going to be questioned all the time, second-guessed, and their motives examined.

Authority is tested all the time. Teachers everywhere talk about the lack of respect, the erosion of what we used to call traditional values. Bosses in the workplace complain that employees don't have the loyalty they used to have. Coaches lament that today's athlete is different from the ones just a decade go, more concerned with individual accomplishments than ever before. You hear about how many parents want to be friends with their kids, not discipline them. Individualism is the new god. Everywhere you look you see the disease of "me," a self-absorption run rampant.

Is it any wonder why it often seems leadership is under attack?

A case in point is the story of Corey Maggete.

In the spring of 1999 Corey was a freshman on the Duke team that lost the national college basketball championship in the final game. By all accounts he is a great young talent, but on a deep team he only averaged something like sixteen minutes a game. Yet shortly after the season ended he announced he was considering leaving Duke after his freshman year to enter the NBA draft, even though Duke coach Mike Krzyzewski advised him not to, telling him that he wasn't ready and he'd be better served by returning to school. As the story goes, Maggete also called Michael Jordan to ask for his advice, Jordan telling him the same thing.

Still, Maggete declared himself eligible for the NBA draft.

This is not meant to denigrate Maggete, yet he's an example of what leaders of young people are facing today. For if some young basketball player at Duke isn't going to listen to Mike Krzyzewski and Michael Jordan, then who is he going to listen to?

Many people don't necessarily want to listen to advice, or at least not from the right people. Nor are they willing to subordinate their individual interests and private agendas for the good of the group. Many of them have come of age in a different era, one in which their first allegiance is to themselves and their careers, not to the company for which they work or the group of which they are a part.

I first discovered this around the third or fourth year in my tenure at Kentucky. I would go into a recruit's home and there would be several people in the room, all in the role of "unofficial adviser." Where there used to be just the parents and maybe the high school coach, now invariably there was the Amateur Athletic Union (AAU) coach, a couple of family friends, an entourage of people ostensibly there to give the kid advice. And more and more the message was that this young man was really only interested in coming to Kentucky for a year or two before going into professional basketball. The idea of this young man coming to Kentucky, maybe paying his dues for a year or two before taking on more of a prominent role? That wasn't even open to discussion. The idea that he might want to come to Kentucky to be a serious student in search of a degree, something to fall back on when the ball stopped bouncing for him? Too often, that didn't even seem to be a consideration.

It became obvious to me that this was the new reality for the elite high school players, this view of college as little more than a springboard to the NBA, this idea that the player was a commodity in which many people had a vested interest. It also became obvious to me that more and more the mind-set was strictly individual-based.

This is today's climate and it transcends basketball, transcends sports. People have no patience, no sense of paying dues or waiting their turn. They want instant gratification, instant rewards, and if they don't get them from you they inevitably will be looking for somewhere else to obtain them. Invariably, they also don't have a lot of discipline either.

But it's pointless to throw up your hands, blame the culture, and say there's nothing you can do about all this. If that's the case, you have no right to be a leader in the first place. Success or failure as a leader depends on how well you can navigate these individual agendas and keep your group's focus clear and consistent. You have to find ways to combat these cultural realities.

One way to do this is to stress the "partnership" approach.

I tell my team all the time that it's like we're shareholders in a company. That company is the Boston Celtics and we all either make it successful or we don't. It's really up to us. And for us to succeed we need teamwork, that none of us can do it alone.

This cannot be stressed enough. As we said in the first chapter, people need to know that your fate is tied to their fate, that you —as the leader—cannot succeed unless they succeed, too.

This is a message I give them during our first meeting together, and one that's repeated consistently. I don't think you can say it enough. Not in today's climate. It's why I talk to my team for ten to fifteen minutes every day. For without this, people's focus quickly wanders. I have players whose moods can change by the hour, never mind the day. They must be constantly reminded what the common goals are.

HANDLE ADVERSITY

There are going to be times when you're not successful. There are going to be times when whatever you do doesn't seem enough, times when you begin to question everything that you're doing because the traditional markers of success are simply not there. There are going to be times when you fail.

This is adversity and you must find a way to not only get through it, but do so in a way that your vision is still intact.

Sometimes you simply cannot be successful at the present time. That's the cold, sobering reality and it happens to everyone sooner or later. It happened to me in 1999.

It was my second year with the Celtics and one to which I had looked forward. Throughout my coaching history the second year always had been a very successful one, the breakout year, the season that was the symbolic turnaround in the program. In my second year at Providence College we came out of mediocrity to go all the way to the Final Four. In my second year with the Knicks we won fifty-two games and the Atlantic Division title. In my second year at Kentucky we were dramatically better than we'd been the first year.

These things simply didn't happen by accident; there were specific reasons for improvement. First and foremost, the system already was in place, the players no longer in culture shock. The work ethic had been established. We already had gone through the transition year, the one that's always the most difficult, so in the second year we picked the fruits of our labor.

I expected the script to be the same with the Celtics.

The year before we had won thirty-six games, a twenty-one-game increase from the year before. Attendance had been up at the FleetCenter, there were many nights when the building had been buzzing, there finally was the feeling that the Celtics had a future and not just a storied past. By all accounts, it had been a very successful first year.

But from the beginning of the second year it almost seemed jinxed.

It was the year of the lockout in the NBA, a work stoppage that had begun July 1st and lasted until January. Not only were we prohibited from talking to players in the off-season, the players also were barred from any NBA workout facility. For a young team like ours, one that's trying to instill a great work ethic in our players and get them to improve in the off-season, this would eventually cripple us. When training camp finally opened in January only two of our players really were ready for the pressing, frenetic style we want to play.

So from the beginning of training camp I knew we were in trouble.

Not that we were the only team with this problem, certainly. But for a young team that relies so much on high energy to be successful, I knew in those first days of training camp that we were nowhere near ready to be successful playing our style—a harbinger that quickly came true as soon as the shortened season began.

The question became: How am I going to deal with it?

I had never been through this before as a coach. Yes, I had sometimes struggled in my first year in a new coaching situation, as I had tried to both implement my vision and start acclimating my players to the methods that eventually were going to get them toward that vision. But never in the second year and never when it appeared as if we already had turned things around, as we had my first year with the Celtics, winning thirty-six games when the Celtics only had won fifteen the year before. I also wasn't used to sensing that the people around me were feeling sorry for me.

So I had to do some soul-searching, too.

And you know what I discovered?

I had to stay focused on my vision for the team.

What I came away with was a stronger belief in my coaching philosophy. At the foundation of this is the belief that you must deserve victory and this is based on first establishing a strong work ethic.

I had seen most of my players report to training camp in marginal shape at best, as if the lessons about hard work and dedication from the year before already had been forgotten. Deserve victory? Hardly. They had strayed from their fundamentals and now they were paying for that. In many ways they had committed one of the original sins: They had forgotten the path that had made them successful in the first place.

And this only made me more secure in my philosophy, more convinced that without working hard and deserving victory we were virtually programming ourselves to fail.

* * *

So how do you handle the challenge of adversity as a leader?

First of all, you need a strategy. Sure, you might want to rant and rave and bemoan your fate. You might want to blame the people who are working for you. That has a short shelf life, though, usually complete with a backlash. Eventually, you have to find a way to get through the adversity as quickly as possible.

You also have to be stronger and more resolute than ever. You are the one to whom others will be looking and if they see panic or doubt in you, then everything only gets worse. You have to be more positive, more visible, more out front with your message.

It's during such times that groups are fragile. They can go in either direction. They can fight through the tough times and eventually be better off for them, or they can succumb, betray all the progress that's already been made, to the point that they end up all but starting over.

Leaders must understand why people win and why they lose. We must learn from our failures, not only to prevent them from becoming a recurring theme, the same repeating over and over, but to know what *not* to do in the future. It became paramount for me as the coach to not only navigate my team through adversity, but also to make them understand why they were losing and what they ultimately could do to change that.

Failure demands explanations and it is up to you as a leader to provide them. There are reasons why companies fail, why teams lose. People must be made aware of them or else they are doomed to repeat them.

This is especially important with young people. They must be made aware that the line between who wins and who loses can be a fine one and that they control it. This is not about wishing and hoping. This is not about trying to get lucky. This is not about waiting for someone else to lose, so you can win by default. This is about taking control of your situation, using your basic fundamentals and skills to impart your will on a situation.

At one point during our struggles in 1999, my assistant coach Jim O'Brien said, "I can't believe you're dealing with this as well as you are."

Jim has been with me for years now, a relationship that dates back to when he first became one of my assistants with the Knicks in 1988. He knows me well.

"If I acted now the way I normally act when I lose we would have tremendous anarchy right now," I told him. "You can't balance success and adversity the same way."

I discovered years ago that if a team is doing well you can work them hard. When a team is winning its collective self-esteem is very high, thus you can demand more of them, be tougher on them. You can push them to limits they didn't believe they can achieve. You almost can't be too tough on them because they can handle anything. All of my successful teams through the years have shared this trait.

Conversely, when a team is losing it's more fragile. Its self-esteem is low, it has no confidence, it fears the future. It doesn't believe in itself. It believes that whatever can go wrong ultimately will go wrong. Thus, you as the leader must deal with them with looser reins. When a team is losing everything gets magnified. Criticism. Doubt. Uncertainty. Fear of failure. Everything.

So my way of dealing with the team during that period of adversity was not to come down hard on them, as much as try to get them to understand why they were not being successful. Losing was bad enough, but losing without realizing the specific reasons for why we were losing was an even greater sin.

My other goal was to convince them that the adversity they were going through now was only going to make us a better team in the future, that we were going to survive this adversity and it was going to make us stronger and hungrier to win; that this was part of the maturation process any group must go through before it truly can be successful. Failure must be treated this way. Not as a stigma, but as a learning tool, something that shows us what not to do.

The problem with the 1999 Celtics was that not enough of my players had been through real adversity before.

This long period of feeling in an overprotected state is what kills a lot of organizations.

If a group doesn't have people who have survived adversity before and it suddenly arrives, people panic. They instantly lose sight of the vision. They lose focus. They lose their patience. They start to dwell on the negatives and get caught up in the short-term. Maybe more significantly, people start looking for ways to save themselves. They look inward. They no longer have faith in the group, so now it's every man for himself.

I saw this start to happen with my Celtics team in 1999. As soon we started to struggle it was like we immediately forgot all the lessons we'd learned the year before. It was like every night was Oscar night. Players started being more concerned with individual performances, their thinking being that, yes, the team is losing but I have to show everyone that it's not my fault. Yes, the season is a huge disappointment, but my career isn't going to suffer because of it.

I had to address this, to try to stop it.

"Here's why you're losing," I told them. "You are all twenty-two years old and you are suffering in this league because of that. You are all twenty-two years old and that is not helping you right now, not in a league where the older, more experienced teams are winning. You are all twenty-two years old and if you could dominate this league at twenty-two then you wouldn't have much of a league. You are all twenty-two and you look at things personally, not collectively, and that is the main reason why you're not successful. You are all twenty-two and if you don't stop caring about your personal stats and your contracts and your individual performances, then you are not going to be successful."

I also told them one more thing:

"There are people telling me we have to get older to be successful, but if you start acting older and stop worrying about your individual statistics, then we are wiser beyond our years."

In speaking to the Knicks' coach Jeff Van Gundy, he was telling me that veteran players don't like to practice, the inference being that younger players do. That's not true. Young players follow the same pattern as older players. Practice is tiring to them because of the eighty-two-game schedule. So I believe it really has nothing to do with age; it's about how much you love your vocation.

* * *

I don't think people know how to get themselves out of a rut. I think they have to be taught how to do this. If they're not, they will revert to all the bad behavior all unsuccessful groups exhibit: They will lie, they will blame others, they will point fingers at others. They will do almost anything to take the onus off themselves.

And this is where leadership comes in.

You have to help them get out of ruts, and you do that by being consistent.

You must constantly be reinforcing your vision, constantly reinforcing the goals of the group, constantly getting the people you're leading to go back to their methods, trying to convince them that by adhering to these methods they ultimately will be successful.

Take Antoine Walker, for example:

During much of the 1999 season he really struggled from the free throw line. Much of foul shooting is practice and endless repetition. The rest is mental. One of the by-products of Antoine's struggling at the line was a loss of confidence, which only made the problem worse. Yet when we wanted him to work with a foul-shooting coach he balked. It was only after we told him that such great NBA players as Danny Manning, Grant Hill, and Glen Rice had used this particular coach did Antoine agree.

You guessed it.

The immediate results were dramatic. He improved greatly in just ten days.

This is why having people around you who have been through adversity before is a decided plus. They know it's something you have to fight through, but that you can survive it and ultimately will be better off for going through it. There's no substitute for experience. People who have not been through adversity before tend to see it as a death march.

What kills a lot of companies is they don't have enough people who are dependable, people who have the wherewithal to withstand adversity. People with character. People who are going to fight through the tough times, with great courage, instead of looking for someone to blame. That's why I do background checks on every person I hire. I want to know as much as I can about their lives, because distracted people are distracted at work, too. People who come out of motivated families tend to be motivated people. People with good work habits and values will bring them to your company, too. And the more people you have with these traits the better chance you have to be successful. This is essential in today's cultural climate.

Still, you must understand that so many things in today's culture are working against you as a leader.

Take this example:

We lost a home game to the New Jersey Nets in the 1999 season. One of the turning points in the game was that Paul Pierce, a rookie at the time, missed two free throws, then came back down the court and blew a defensive assignment because he was upset at himself for missing the two free throws. What upset me was certainly not that Paul had missed the two free throws, but that he had let that affect his defensive performance, especially after it happened shortly after a time-out during which we had stressed what we were going to do defensively. So afterward I expressed my displeasure to him in the locker room in no uncertain teams.

That night we flew out to a future away game. I was still upset at Paul, at what I perceived to be one more example of us being victimized by a young player letting his immaturity show. These were the things that were killing us and I had taken some of my frustration out on Paul. At one point on the flight Paul came up to me and said, "Will you stop beating this dead horse with a stick?"

I laughed.

"You're right," I said. "That's the last time we'll mention it."

So I figured it was over, right?

Wrong.

Shortly afterward Paul went into a slump, not playing nearly as well as he had previously, something which is standard practice for a rookie. But in one of the Boston papers was a story —quoting an anonymous source—that said Paul's slump was directly related to me chewing him out in the locker room after the loss to New Jersey for missing the two free throws. What should have been an isolated incident took on a life of its own, having ramifications that far transcended its actual importance.

Yet, I knew I had contributed to this, too. In retrospect, my mistake was taking my frustration out on Paul in the locker room after the loss to New Jersey. What I should have done was wait until the next morning's practice and then made the larger point that what Paul had done was something that *everyone* was doing—making mental mistakes.

That's something Hubie Brown was very good at when I worked for him with the New York Knicks for two years in the early eighties. He rarely brought his displeasure into the locker room after a loss, at a time when emotions often run high and no one is happy, the time when it's easy to say things you really don't want to say. Instead, he would save it for practice the following day, when the passions of the moment had cooled.

That's what I should have done. If I had, the situation never would have occurred.

TREAT PEOPLE FAIRLY

One of the ways to be consistent is to treat people fairly.

I tell my players that my door is always open if they want to talk to me. Why are they not playing as much as they think they should? Why is someone playing ahead of them? Why does it seem like I have little faith in them? I will answer these questions.

I don't want them guessing. I don't want them hearing things third-hand, distorted messages. I want them to hear it from me. I tell them, "You may not like what you hear, but you will hear the truth."

People want that.

They want the truth, they want to be treated fairly, and they want consistency. They don't want variables, things always changing. They want to know what's going to happen, to believe that things are going to be fair.

Case in point:

We began the 1999–2000 season with Adrian Griffin as one of our starters.

Who is Adrian Griffin?

That's a good question. Because heading into training camp odds are that not too many people knew who Adrian Griffin was. He graduated from Seton Hall in 1996, someone who had a good college career, but by no means a great one. At six foot five he was considered a classic NBA "tweener," too small to really be a forward, not quick enough to be an off-guard. He wasn't drafted by the NBA and spent the next couple of years knocking around on the lower levels of professional basketball. And though he was the MVP of the CBA in 1999, the doubts about him were still there.

But we brought him into our rookie camp in the summer and he just grew on our coaching staff, one of those players who is not flashy, but plays without ego and does all the little things right. The more we saw him the more we liked him, so we signed him later in the summer. Still, he was the lowest-paid player on our team and no one probably figured he was going to see a lot of playing time.

In our first meeting, though, I told our team that the players who bought in to what we were trying to do were the ones who were going to play, independent of their salary status or other variables. And when Danny Fortson got hurt and we were looking for someone to replace him in the starting lineup, it was the consensus of the coaching staff it should be Griffin. If nothing else, it was a reaffirmation we were going to be both fair and consistent in what we said at our first meeting.

TAKE THE HEAT

Being criticized—fairly or not—comes with the territory and is part of your professional diet.

When I first began coaching at Boston University my style of play was immediately criticized. My style was to press all over the court, to run and trap and play up-tempo. From the beginning there were people who said that style couldn't be successful over the long haul, they said it was a gamble defense,they said it would wear my players out, they said it was a gimmick. They even said that my players eventually would get sick of playing that way and that other players would not want to come play in that style.

No matter that we were successful, essentially proving these criticisms wrong. Throughout my head coaching career—a journey that took me to Providence College, to the New York Knicks, to Kentucky—those criticisms never really went away. To some extent, they've always been there, lurking beneath the surface, ready to spring out anytime there's adversity.

You must understand, though, that, as a leader, criticism is here to stay, that it's part of your job. So prepare yourself for it.

You also must understand that people today tend to be very sensitive to any kinds of criticism. An off-hand comment. A cutting remark. The wrong thing at the wrong time. All these things can lead to overreaction, which can strain the ability to lead.

Another thing to remember is that you will be scrutinized like never before. It's simply the tenor of the times. From the media, to the people you are leading, to the public, they will all be looking at you under a microscope, just waiting for those flaws to appear, whether they are personal or professional. Leaders today live in a fishbowl and have to be like Caesar's wife—above suspicion.

Even if you are, though, you still will be criticized. No one is immune. Look at all the great leaders in history. All had people who opposed them. All had people who wanted them to fail. All had people who doubted them, questioned them. All had enemies. It simply comes with the territory. And the more public your position is the more you will be criticized.

Can you handle unwarranted criticism?

Some people can't, especially the first time it happens to them. They are simply not emotionally ready to handle it. They want to strike back, retaliate. They want everyone to know the criticism is unfair, wrong. It begins to dominate their professional life, taking up much more time than it should.

Interestingly, you often see this with successful people in industry that get involved in professional sports teams. These people all have been tremendously successful, but often they're not used to being under the kind of media scrutiny that professional sports teams are under. They start to get taken over the coals on the sports page or on the sports talk shows and they can't believe it. They don't know how to react.

In their book, *The Leadership Lessons of Jesus*, authors Bob Briner and Ray Pritchard tell the story of tennis great Arthur Ashe, who worked very hard as the president of the Association of Tennis Players to help the players who were not great stars, those who often lost in the early rounds of tournaments. Yet many of these players verbally attacked Ashe in a pre-Wimbledon players' meeting one year and the unwarranted criticism greatly upset Ashe. Never again did he put himself in a leadership position that could subject him to that kind of attack.

But criticism is part of being a leader.

I first learned this in New York as an assistant to Hubie Brown with the Knicks. When it started to go badly for him Hubie would read everything and it ate him up inside. Someone would question him and it would bother him. He took it hard and I understand why he did. From a coaching standpoint he knew he was right, but it didn't matter. You can't answer writers. They're like echoes.

So when I became the Knicks coach in the summer of 1987 I knew what to expect. New York is the kind of town that will boo you on your wedding night if you lose. I used to tell my players then that you can't play in New York if you are bothered by people knocking you or even making things up.

And the worst part of criticism?

When you know the criticism is wrong. Rest assured, that's going to happen, too. You are going to be criticized and sometimes that criticism is going to be misguided. When that happens, you simply must realize that it's part of the business you're in and there's really nothing you can do about it.

When I get criticized—either in the newspapers or on talk radio—my strategy is not to deal with it. I learned that in New York, too. I soon realized it was simply easier not to read it. That way I could deal with people professionally and objectively and not be influenced by what they might have written the day before. For the most part it worked and I've taken that lesson with me. I don't read it, I don't listen to it, nor do I want the people around me to tell me what's being written or said. Sometimes, though, that's impossible. During those times when I'm aware of the criticism I do my best to ignore it. And even if I can't, I'm not going to let it effect me.

A couple of days before the 1999–2000 season started there was an article in the *Providence Journal* by Mike Szostak on our upcoming season, titled "Celts Season Over Before It Starts." I did not see the article, but several people told me about it. In fact, on my coach's show, that's aired on WBZ in Boston, the host Bob Lobel asked me about it. My reaction? To defuse it. I said that particular writer had every right to say what he did. That his job is to have an opinion and be able to present it and that even though I might not agree with it, I have no problem with that kind of story as long as that person has his name attached to it, for how can you have a problem with someone's opinion?

What people write, and what they say on the radio, is not going to change the way I lead. I am going to be consistent. I am going to be true to my values and beliefs.

REINFORCE GOOD HABITS

A leader must also reinforce good habits.

Take Dwayne Schintzius, for example:

He is a seven-foot-three player, a former first-round draft pick, who has bounced around the NBA. We signed him before the start of the 1998–'99 season, essentially taking a chance on him, and then he was a part of the Ron Mercer trade the following summer. When we got him, though, we soon discovered he had a major self-esteem problem. In training camp, Schintzius said he hurt. I told him that he should hurt, that when you come into training camp as a professional athlete and you're not in shape you should hurt. If you run the race you should be tired. But you also should be gratified. Because you've done something for yourself.

One day Lester Conner, a former NBA player who is in his first year as my assistant with the Celtics, said he'd been up all night watching film.

"How was it?" I asked.

"I loved it," he said, "but I'm tired."

"You're supposed to be tired," I said. "You just spent all night watching film. You should be tired."

In both these examples, I was trying to reinforce these good habits, to make both Dwayne and Lester aware that changing behavior is often difficult, they they were heading in the right direction.

As the leader, you must constantly be reinforcing the goals of the group.

Take the NBA work stoppage in 1999. Too many of the players failed to come back in great shape. Instead, they treated their time off as one long summer vacation that was never going to end, like ten year olds at summer camp. Instead of working extra hard to stay in shape, they used the excuse that 1) there probably wouldn't be a season anyway, and 2) if there was a season they would have plenty of time to play themselves into shape.

The work stoppage created bad habits.

You must always be looking for bad habits, for bad habits always are going to spring up: the person who starts taking shortcuts, the ones who start to take things for granted, the person who starts to embrace success. The ones who forget the vision. These are all common failings and you always have to be looking for them, to nip them in the bud and prevent them from becoming ingrained.

Sports is a terrific microcosm of human behavior.

When a team is going well, it's sort of a classic example of teamwork and selflessness. People have a shared vision and common goals. They depend on one another and everyone benefits from the success of the group. You watch them play and these traits become very obvious.

Conversely, when a team is not going well you tend to see the breakdown of these traits. People revert to individual agendas. They lose sight of the vision. You start to see the bad habits.

And the interesting thing about sports?

Both of these examples can happen in the same game.

But don't kid yourself. This same scenario takes place in every business there is, even if it's over an extended period of time and not as noticeable. People are forever drifting into bad habits, for a variety of reasons. So you must constantly be vigilant.

Your rule is simple: Reinforce good habits and nip bad ones in the bud.

Good habits are being team-oriented, being unselfish, putting the group ahead of yourself. Bad habits are not working hard, being self-absorbed, quitting, beating your own drum, being selfish, resting on your laurels, taking things for granted.

All these things are distractions, they get in the way of you building your team and they must constantly be addressed. If you look at any group that's struggling—any team, any business—invariably you will find people that are more concerned with their own performance rather than the group's, and the propensity to point fingers and blame others.

So you must constantly be vigilant when you see these habits.

I do this all the time. Virtually every day we show our players clips of them taking shots. What's a good shot? What's a bad shot? These things are constantly gone over, examined. As a coaching staff, we don't want these things to go unnoticed.

In a business, you can take similar actions: Be in daily contact with employees, keep your door open, give a consistent message of your vision for them, let them know what they're doing right and what they're doing wrong.

And just as people get themselves into trouble by reverting back to their bad habits, leaders can get themselves into trouble, too.

How?

By becoming distracted. By answering their critics. By not being there. By doing things that lose people's trust. In short, by losing consistency. That message that seemed so clear and direct in the beginning has gotten lost along the way.

As a leader, I am always looking for consistency from the people who work for me. I want players I know are going to play defense every night. I want players I know are always going to give me a great effort. I want assistants I can rely on. And just as I want consistency from the people that work for me, I know they want consistency from me, too.

KEY CHAPTER POINTS

- **Handle Adversity** There are going to be times when you are not successful, times when whatever you do it doesn't seem to be enough. This is adversity and you must find a way to get through it, for sometimes you simply can't be successful. During these times, you must keep adhering to your beliefs. You have to be stronger and more resolute than ever. You are the one others will be looking toward for leadership, so you have to be more positive, more visible, more up front with your message.

- **Treat People Fairly** One of the best ways to be consistent is to treat people fairly. People don't like vagueness and things that always are changing. They don't want to hear things third-hand, distorted messages. They want to know what is going to happen, to believe that things are going to be treated fairly.

- **Take the Heat** You are going to be criticized. You are going to be second-guessed. It's simply the tenor of the times. No one is immune. So you must be able to handle criticism, even if it's unwarranted.

- **Reinforce Good Habits** You must constantly be reinforcing good habits, just as you should constantly be reinforcing the goals of the group. You must always be looking for bad habits or people who are looking for shortcuts, or else others who are either taking things for granted or embracing success.

POPE JOHN PAUL II

Despite our tendency to think of great leaders as being big, strong, and imposing figures, the reality is they come in all shapes and sizes. The actual physical size of an individual doesn't seem to play a particularly important role in whether or not a person stands out as a great leader. A weak person who happens to have a commanding presence isn't going to become a successful leader. Conversely, a small person with a big heart can become one.

Certainly, Pope John Paul II doesn't quite fit our image of a great leader. He is small and frail, almost delicate to the point that when he's in the midst of a huge crowd, we tend to worry about his safety. In those situations, he reminds us of a flower caught in a dangerous whirlwind.

But if ever there was a case where appearances are deceiving, this is it. While Pope John Paul II may be getting up in years, and he may be small in stature, the fact is he's as tough and courageous and steadfast as any great leader in history. And like those leaders, he is a man who stands firmly on the principles, ideals, and traditions in which he so passionately believes.

Being a religious leader is a much different proposition than being a political leader, or any other kind of leader, for that matter. Religious leaders are bound by tradition, by certain tenets that have been handed down to them through the years. Strict adherence to doctrine is at the very heart of any religious organization. Without it, no church can survive.

As head of the Roman Catholic Church, Pope John Paul II is the spiritual leader to millions of people throughout the world. He is their beacon of light, their ray of hope. It is through him that their prayers flow.

When you stop and think about it, the challenges facing the pope are unlike those faced by any other leader. For one thing, his followers literally cover the globe. And they are vastly different in so many ways. A Catholic in Ireland isn't at all like a Catholic in Argentina. Virtually nothing about them is the same. Language, way of life, traditions . . . all completely different. They may as well live on different planets. And yet, a common thread links them and that thread is the Roman Catholic Church.

No pope lives in static times. Things are always changing and most of the time, those changes come swiftly. Think about how the world has changed just in the past twenty-five years. It's mind-boggling. Some of the changes have been for the better, some haven't been. Many, especially in the medical field, have been controversial to say the least.

Because of these changes, Pope John Paul II has been forced to deal with situations and face challenges that none of his predecessors could have imagined. Birth control, legalized abortion, artificial fertilization, euthanasia, the death penalty . . . these are issues that have really only come to the forefront of public debate in the past quarter century. And almost without exception, the voices on either side are loud and, all too often, violent.

That Pope John Paul II has weathered so many storms while consistently becoming more and more beloved by his followers is a remarkable tribute to the man and to his abilities as a leader. Most leaders, regardless of how strongly their constituents feel about them, sooner or later tend to wear out their welcome. Or they are discarded when the times change and their ideas are no longer embraced. Not so with Pope John Paul II. His popularity grows with each passing year.

Why? As someone fortunate enough to have met Pope John Paul II, I can say that a big reason is because he is a person who inspires confidence in people. When you walk away from him, you feel better about yourself and your own faith. That's because his faith flows through him and into you. You are lifted on his shoulders. It's a rare gift when a leader can do that.

Another reason why he's such a successful leader is his great ability to communicate his message. He's obviously a very intelligent man, but being intelligent wouldn't be enough if he lacked the ability to clearly articulate his theological message. Pope John Paul II possesses that ability in abundance.

What's particularly impressive is the way he can inspire people of all ages. You would think that, because of his advanced age, young people might tune him out. They don't. In fact, the opposite is true. Pope John Paul II is extremely popular with younger Catholics. That is due in no small part to his charm and charisma. Even when you disagree with what he says, you like him.

Few world leaders in this century have demonstrated more courage, compassion, and conviction than Pope John Paul II. This is a man who had the courage to stand his ground against the mighty Soviet Union and back the Solidarity movement in Poland at a time when communism was still a world threat. His bold stance helped bring down the wall of Communist tyranny. For that, he will be go down as one of the twentieth century's most important figures.

Compassion? He visited the man who shot and almost killed him. How many of us could be that magnanimous, that compassionate toward someone who tried to end our life? I doubt that many of us could find it in our heart to be so forgiving. But he could, and it was an act of great significance.

Pope John Paul II is by far the most-traveled pope of all time. That's another thing that endears him to so many people. It's one thing to sit in the Vatican and say you understand the plight of people in Third World countries, but it's another thing to actually visit them and see up close what the situation is.

But of all the traits that make Pope John Paul II a great

leader, none is more important than his *conviction*. He knows in his heart what is right and wrong and nothing is going to persuade him otherwise. He not only has conviction, he also has the moral and spiritual courage to follow those convictions. He simply will not bend to the wishes of angry dissenters or to what is currently popular or "in."

And make no mistake, some of his decisions are unpopular, especially in this country, where he's taken real flack on the issues of abortion, birth control, and the ordination of women priests. But no matter how loud the protests are, he refuses to back down. His conviction is matched by his fearlessness.

Pope John Paul II has had to navigate some choppy seas during his years as head of the Roman Catholic Church. He has been tested to the limit, spiritually and physically, and he has never once wavered or faltered. His love and his inner strength are boundless.

8

MAINTAIN FOCUS

In order to stay on top, leaders must keep their focus.

This sounds simple, but for many leaders, it's their toughest challenge.

People lose focus all the time. Groups lose focus. Companies lose focus.

Look at Kodak, which dominated film for so long that they began to believe they never could be caught, until the technology changed and hurt them considerably. Look at IBM, which also was slow to deal with changing technology. In a sense, they both lost the fundamentals that made them successful in the first place.

Companies do this all the time and people do this all the time.

For example, take the person who becomes successful after years of hard work. Let's say that for years he played golf on Saturday mornings. That was his time away from the ringing telephone and the demands of work. Away from his family. Those four hours every Saturday morning were his little sanctuary, his personal reward for all the hard work and long hours he spent at his job.

Now, though, he feels like he deserves another reward. Because he's worked hard and he's been successful, right? So he adds another round of golf on Wednesday afternoons. And that's eventually followed by another round of golf on Friday afternoons, too. This becomes another day he leaves work early, another day he rewards himself.

So what began innocently enough as one round of golf a week on Saturday morning, the reward for all his hard work, has now turned into three rounds of golf a week. What began as something peripheral to his week has now become a significant part of his life.

You see this a lot with college coaches who've become very successful. Usually, this has taken a long time to accomplish, a lot of years and a lot of work, summers spent either recruiting or working summer camps, a lot of years of paying dues. Long hours and few vacations: the long road people travel to become successful. Then they reach their mountaintop and so often many of them simply don't want to work so hard anymore. They feel they shouldn't have to. To the victor belongs the spoils, right? Now the first thing they do is they take more time off. They see this as something they're entitled to, a payback for all their hard work, so they don't recruit as hard. They don't make that extra call. They don't put in as many hours. They don't interrupt their vacation to go to that summer camp where many of the best recruits are, like they did when they were on the way up, dreaming of getting to the top. They rely more and more on their assistant coaches to do what they used to do. They don't go the extra mile the way they used to.

And what is it that invariably happens?

Their performance starts to suffer.

Why?

Because they've lost that eye of the tiger, the focus that made them so successful in the first place. They've lost those fundamentals. And when you lose your fundamentals the result is both a soft body and a soft mind.

You see it with companies who have become very successful. They have had great vision and have seen it actualized. They have grown and prospered, reached a height that once would have been unimaginable. Then they get complacent, begin to luxuriate in their own success. In very subtle ways they aren't as hungry anymore. They get fat. They get lazy. And eventually things begin to change. Eventually, they begin to get caught by their competition, the ones that still are hungry, still are trying to get to the top of the mountaintop.

MAINTAIN DISCIPLINE

Why do people lose their focus?

Many reasons. A lack of fundamentals. Boredom. Complacency. The feeling they need another challenge. It's human nature.

It's at these times of success when you have to work at being more focused.

Focus is a discipline. You can train yourself to get better at it, just as you can train yourself to work harder, be more organized, and manage your time better. Now you also can learn to recognize those times when focus can be very fragile. Three situations immediately come to mind:

The first is when the newness wears off. You often see that with kids in school. They go back in September full of good intentions. They begin the school year by being organized, keeping up with their homework, swept along by their good intentions. Then about a month into it, they hit the wall. The newness is gone. They begin to slide back into their old habits. That sharp sense of focus they began the school year with is already gone.

People do this all the time, whether it's with diets, New Year's resolutions, fitness programs, a renewed commitment to their jobs, whatever. They begin with great intentions, ride that for a while, and then start to slide. Once the newness wears off, focus will start to wear off, too.

The second? When there has been a success.

The example is people on diets. They are disciplined and organized, see results, then figure they can reward themselves. Haven't they been good? Hasn't the diet worked? Don't they deserve a hot fudge sundae every once in a while? Can't they take a few days off from their diet? Don't they deserve this?

You don't have to be Columbo to see the obvious trap. These people have embraced success. And once that happens their focus will suffer, too.

The third situation where focus starts to slip is when you simply don't have the time. During those periods when you feel as if you're being pulled in a hundred different directions it's easy to get overwhelmed and lose focus. There are too many things on your plate and there's no way you can do justice to all of them, right?

A good example of this is with my own job:

When I became the president of the Celtics in May of 1997, there was some speculation that I was in uncharted territory, that though I was a successful coach I had never really run an organization before. I didn't believe this. I always had considered myself the director of Kentucky basketball, that even though we had an athletic director at the University of Kentucky, my responsibility was the basketball program and that was similar to running a company. I had media demands, public relations demands, constant demands on my time. In essence, I was doing everything a CEO would do, except without the title.

One of the false impressions I had when I first came to the Celtics, though, was that there was a lack of leadership at the top, and that I was going to have to overhaul the entire organization. That was the assumption I brought with me to the job, but it was a wrong one.

I soon realized that I didn't have to integrate a whole new corporate strategy and that so many things were already in place: the sales people, the marketing people, the people who handled community service. These things were running well, so there was no reason to change them. The best thing I could do was to step back and let these people continue to do what they already were doing.

That was a major plus. Still, I have obvious time constraints. First and foremost, I have to make the Celtics a better basketball team. Everything else is subordinate to that. It's analogous to opening a new restaurant. Yes, you need the dining room to have the right ambiance, and the waitpeople to be efficient and professional. Yes, you want a great location. But while these things may get you initial business, if your food is sub-par all these things eventually become irrelevant.

So I went to the people in marketing, the people in promotion, the people in the various departments, and said, "Here's how I can help you. These are my skills and it's up to you to utilize them. I can't tell you how to do it, but here's the time I have, here are the skills I have, and you have to tell me what to do."

Doing that accomplished two things:

It not only showed these people in the various departments that I had faith in them, but it also allowed me to maintain my focus. Instead of being pulled in many different directions, I was able to focus in on the task at hand.

As the leader of the Celtics, it is important for me to communicate focus to those I lead: I make myself available to our marketing and promotional people whenever possible. Often, I will meet groups of season ticket holders before home games in the FleetCenter. Sometimes it's for only a few minutes, but I feel that these things are imperative. My rule is simple: I will go anywhere, and do anything, to promote the Boston Celtics.

Here is what we did with Citizen's Bank, for example:

Citizen's had a problem in Boston. They were dominated in the Boston market by Fleet and Bank of Boston, so they wanted some kind of tie-in with the Celtics to increase their visibility in the area.

Citizen's flew me to Newport, Rhode Island, where I spoke

to several of the bank's key people. I gave them copies of my third book, *Success Is a Choice*, so that they could be aware of what was at the core of my philosophy. I also stressed the fact that they could improve their place in the Boston market by identifying with the Celtics, even though the Celtics play in the FleetCenter, a building named after Fleet, one of the largest banks in the region. They signed me to a personal services contract, which included me doing some TV commercials, and we began the partnership between Citizen's Bank and the Boston Celtics.

When we began, Citizens had an 8 percent name recognition in Boston. In just three months it jumped to 38 percent, and in one year they were regarded as having one of the greatest rises in banking in New England. The Celtics benefited by some clever advertising that helped keep the team in the public eye, something that we always must be trying to do, since we cannot take for granted that people always are thinking of us just because we are the Celtics and have been playing basketball in Boston for over half a century.

This was the start of a great partnership. Citizen's had great leadership, vision, and they had the banking fundamentals in place; we helped their recognition factor and kept our team out there as well.

* * *

Another important thing to remember is the tougher the times the more you have to focus. A leader is never needed more than in times of crisis. History tells us this, from Churchill to Roosevelt, from Kennedy during the Cuban missile crisis to Martin Luther King Jr. telling African Americans that he had a dream for them. There is something very comforting about a leader telling us that yes, things are difficult right now, but we're going to get through them. It's the essence of leadership, from the great figures of history to parents comforting a young child.

The message is the same: We will survive this; things will get better. And the subtle message? During such times it is the leader who is both calm and soothing, the leader who has taken control of the situation. The leader who is going to show us the way.

The more people are losing their heads around you, the more you must keep yours.

When we were going through our adversity with the Celtics in the winter of 1999 I knew that if I got down, or overreacted, then things would have been worse. I knew my team was emotionally fragile, that they weren't ready to handle the ramifications of their failure; that they needed me to help them navigate their way through it. They were young and many had never gone through this kind of adversity before. Take Antoine Walker, for example: Here's someone who had been a high school All-American basketball player, had won an NCAA title as a college sophomore, had been an NBA lottery pick shortly after, and had been signed to a seventy-million-dollar contract. And now he was being booed in the FleetCenter every time he missed a shot. Nothing had prepared him for that. Nothing could have prepared him for that.

So my message to him during this difficult stretch was that he had to resort to his fundamentals, concentrate on rebounding and playing better defense, on taking higher percentage shots and doing things to make his teammates better.

That's what you must stress to the people you are leading. When adversity strikes you must return to your fundamentals. Make it simple. Establish more short-term goals. Rediscover your basics. Do everything you can do to get people to believe again, that these tough times are merely a blip on the radar screen, certainly nothing that's going to last.

The other thing you must stress to people is that none of us can rest on our laurels. Just as it doesn't matter to those people booing Antoine Walker in the FleetCenter what his past accomplishments, it also no longer matters what my coaching résumé is either. This is a mistake people make all the time.

Your résumé gets you the job, but that résumé gets filed once you start that job. You might want people to respect your past, to give you some slack because of it. They won't. That's just the way it is, both in business and in life. You can say that's not fair and you may be right. But it's irrelevant. The only thing that counts is what you do now. Your reputation only means something on Old Timer's Day.

We all are one-day contracts.

In a sense, I've always operated that way. I was born in Manhattan, spent my childhood in Queens, then later lived on Long Island. I've always experienced new people and new places. I like going to different places on vacations. I like new challenges, to always be testing myself.

But whether you're this way or not, rest assured that people always are evaluating you, regardless of what you've accomplished in the past. What have you done for me lately? That's the old cliché, but it's also true.

We see this in sports all the time. It's been said that everyone ends up in the transactions section of the sports page sooner or later, even the greats. That's the record of who was traded, or cut, or waived. In a sense, it's an athlete's obituary page, the place where everyone's career ends. Even the great players get old. Even the great players reach a point when it no longer matters what they did.

That's a good lesson for all of us, too.

All of us are constantly under a microscope. Have we lost a step? Have we grown lazy? Have we embraced success? Have we lost that eye of the tiger? Have the times passed us by? Not to think that we are being evaluated that way is naive. People are constantly making judgments on us all the time, fairly or unfairly.

That knowledge alone should be enough to make us maintain our focus.

AVOID DISTRACTIONS

Not that this should come as any great surprise, but young people will tend to lose focus very quickly.

They have grown up in an instant gratification culture, one ruled by the television clicker. They have been all but programmed to have short attention spans, courtesy of video games, television, movies, and now the Internet, all of which distract them with special effects and a kind of visual "magic" to which other generations were less exposed. They have come of age in a culture that's frenetic, constantly bombarded by noise and changing images.

Many kids have played on a variety of youth league teams. They have played for innumerable coaches, who often have coddled them and reinforced the notion that they essentially can do anything they want. Individual stats are very important to them. Individual accomplishments are very important to them, as are individual awards. They also tend to be very sensitive to any kind of criticism. What we might see as coaching, they perceive to be criticism.

Young people also have a difficult time envisioning the future, tending to live only in the present tense, not thinking about consequences. That's simply a part of being young, the feeling that you are going to be young forever. The future? It might as well be on the other side of the moon as far as they're concerned. In basketball terms, the next basket, the next game; these are their frames of reference, not any vision of the future. To them, practice is often a burden.

Selflessness, discipline: These often are virtues they don't have. This is not surprising. They have grown up as the center of their own universes.

Often, the best thing for young people to do is fail. They almost need to go through hardship as part of the maturation process.

It's like Antoine Walker referring to himself as a veteran

All-Star after only being in the NBA two years. Why did he make such a ridiculous statement, one that could come back to haunt him?

Simple.

He's young. The key is for Antoine not to make the mistake again, not the mistake itself.

Yet it doesn't do any good for me to say, "I can't understand how he can say something like that. I just can't fathom it." Nor does it do any good for anyone in a leadership position to say they can't fathom certain behavior from young people.

Well, fathom it.

Because it's not going away. Young people are going to say inappropriate things. They are going to do things that are misguided, things that make you shake your head and wonder why. They are going to have times when they appear distracted and unfocused. You must understand that and deal with the ramifications. There is absolutely no substitute for experience. Not to recognize that is self-delusion.

We have all seen talented people who never seem to live up to their potential for some reason or the other: the salesman who never seems to live up to the promise of his first years, the gifted athlete whose career seems to plateau. People who have great early success often later fade into oblivion, drifting and moving from one thing to another, seemingly unable to make the kind of commitment necessary for long-term success.

It's a trait that you often see in people who always seem to be changing careers. Invariably, they start out with good intentions, are enthusiastic about their job, and for a while feed off the momentum caused by that enthusiasm. Then something happens. The newness wears off, their excitement wanes, and their performance starts declining.

This is what happens when you lose focus and it manifests itself in all kinds of ways.

So how do you deal with it?

Let's take an extreme example:

Let's say I learn that someone on my staff is having personal problems. Unless I'm asked, this is not something I want to deal with. It's that person's business. I do meet the spouses of the people I hire, for I want to know if they are upbeat, positive people. But that's usually as far as I go. I don't want to be Big Brother. I don't want to create an atmosphere where the people who work for me feel I'm being intrusive, crossing boundaries they don't want me to cross. I don't want to delve into things that are personal.

So my message to this person who is having personal problems is simple and direct: When you come into the workplace you must leave your personal life behind.

You must come to work and program your mind so that you are focused on the task at hand. This is your responsibility, regardless of what's going on in your personal life. This is your job and when you're on the job all your attention, all your energy, must go to that job. Everything else must be blocked out. When you cross those lines it's all business. That's what being a professional is all about.

That is what I'm constantly trying to get across to my young team, this concept of what it takes to be a professional. Being a professional basketball player is more than simply getting paid for playing. It's about being on time. It's about having a great work ethic. It's about having a positive attitude. It's about not quitting when adversity shows up on your doorstep. It's about having goals, both short-term ones and long-term ones. It's about being committed to the group of which you are a part.

It's also what focus is all about.

People must continually be reminded of their fundamentals, the building blocks of what they do. Look at the way a golfer takes practice swings before he actually hits the ball. Sure, some of this is simply loosening up. On a deeper, level, though, it's an instant refresher course, a quick inventory through the mechanics of a golf swing. A PGA golfer doesn't just walk up and hit the ball in a big tournament, relying on muscle memory and his natural ability. He is always concerned about his fundamentals, remaining in focus. Basketball players don't simply walk out of the locker room and begin playing a game. They stretch. They take layups to get loose. They take practice shots in search of a good rhythm. They are constantly rechecking their fundamentals.

It's a great lesson for all of us.

* * *

Another way to maintain focus is to maintain your passion. Passion can make up for a lot of other ills.

People who are passionate about what they do are great to be around. They boost morale, make the workplace a better place to be. In short, they inflate the people around them. Compare them to the people who have no passion, the ones who give off the vibes that work is always some incredible burden.

Negative people suck the air out of everyone around them. Just as a positive attitude rubs off on everyone, so do pessimism and cynicism. These attitudes are morale killers. They affect your organization every day.

As a leader, you always are looking for upbeat, positive people, people who are passionate about what they do.

As the Celtics struggled during the shortened 1999 season the question that I was continually asked was if I regretted leaving Kentucky to come to the Celtics. I had had great success at Kentucky and yet I had chosen to leave all that in the spring of 1997 for the great challenge of trying to rebuild the Celtics. Why wouldn't I be asked this? And if I wasn't getting the question, my friends were. The assumption was that since we were struggling I obviously had made a bad decision and that if I could instantly clap my hands and stamp my feet and be back in Kentucky—like some basketball version of Dorothy in *The Wizard of Oz*—I would certainly do it.

That assumption couldn't be more wrong.

I remember once asking Cawood Leford, the longtime broadcaster of Kentucky basketball games, if he ever thought about how far he'd come from growing up in a small Kentucky town, and he answered by saying, "No, I never do. The time for looking back is when you're retired sitting on the porch. Then you can look back. Not before."

I feel the same way.

Throughout my career I have never looked back. I make a decision about the future and I move into it. Yes, there are many cherished memories in the places I've been, but this is not the time to dwell on them. What motivates me are challenges and I have a huge one: to try to hang another championship banner in the rafters of the FleetCenter and restore the Celtics to their past glory.

This is what motivates me. It keeps me young. It keeps me wanting to come to work every day. It keeps me squarely in the moment, which is where I want to live. Not in the musty past where you sit alone with your memories, as cherished as they might be. There will be time enough for that. Maintaining my passion for what I do keeps me focused. It keeps me working hard, keeps my discipline. Living in the present tense, consumed with what you're doing, is what keeps you focused. Regardless of what happens in my career with the Celtics, I see this as a wonderful opportunity.

ALWAYS BE PREPARED

Imagine a professional football team that shows up to play the big game on Sunday afternoon without practicing during the week, the assumption being that simply because the players are going to try hard in the game and do their best to win that that should be enough.

Ridiculous?

Of course. Any coach who did this would be drummed out of the business in a week.

But many people treat their jobs like this, as if they can simply show up and that's enough.

Being prepared is a big part of being focused.

It's surprising how many people don't prepare. They work
hard, they're committed to their jobs, and they care about their
performance, yet they don't do the necessary preparation needed
to ensure success, as if they figure they're either going to get by
on their talent alone, or things are somehow simply going to
work out. As a leader, you must understand this:

You can never prepare too much.

The people who arrive at the workplace thirty seconds before they're scheduled to begin work, harried and rushed, have
not properly prepared. The boss who walks into the sales meeting without planning what he wants to accomplish during that
meeting has not properly prepared. The clothing store that does
not have enough sales people on staff has not prepared. These are
all examples of forgetting fundamentals and when fundamentals
are not constantly reinforced, both people and groups will lose
focus.

So much of your success happens before the actual event.
It's the homework you do before the test, the studying you do before the sales presentation, the constant rehearsal before the play
opens on Broadway. You see this all the time. The teams that
practice well during the week invariably play well on the weekend. The salesman who knows his customers has an edge. The
company that knows its market does better than the company
that doesn't. This is common sense.

In the first chapter of this book we discussed beginning to
impart your vision in the first chapter, the importance of making
a good first impression.

Implicit in that was that I had gone into the first meeting
with the Celtics prepared, knowing what I wanted to say, aware
of possible questions, emotionally ready to take care of the situation. I had played out this scene endless times in my mind, a
way of visualization. There was nothing that could have come up

for which I didn't think I would have been ready. Imagine how different that first meeting can be if you're not prepared, if you figure you can simply show up and wing it.

That's why I believe so much in practice.

Most people would be amazed at the amount of preparation we do before every game. We scout the other team. We break down film on them. We know their offensive sets. We know their defensive tendencies. We know their out-of-bounds plays. We break down the individuals on the other team, to the point that we know their games inside and out. Then we provide this information to our players. We go over it. We do everything we can think of to put us in a position to be able to win the game. This happens eighty-two games a year. Our competition does the same thing. Not to guarantee that we are going to win it, understand, but to have a *chance* to win it.

That is what focus is.

It's not a luxury. It's not something you can turn on and off according to your whim. Focus is a necessity, an essential part of the leadership profile.

There always are going to be days when you know your group is going to struggle. Just as individuals are going to have off days, and times when they want to coast, so do groups. That's when you need focus more than ever.

For example:

I know that during a season there are going to be days in practice when it's going to be a struggle. It might be because we won a game the night before, and everyone is feeling good about themselves, embracing success. It might be that we're coming off the road and the guys are tired. Whatever the reason, I know the potential exists for this to be a wasted day, one of those days when everyone seems to simply be going through the motions. This is when the group needs to be reminded of their focus more than ever.

On such days my message to them is that we are going to be here anyway, so why don't we make the best of it? Why should we be content to simply go through the motions? Why should we just mail in our performance? Why shouldn't we just work as hard as we can, give the best performance we can, and then we'll get out of here for the day? On such days I may even make a deal with my players—namely, that if they collectively give a great effort I will shorten practice.

The key is to keep everyone focused as often as possible for focus is what gets you through the tough times. Focus is what keeps everyone pointing to a common goal. Focus is whether your original vision is going to get actualized.

KEY CHAPTER POINTS

- **Maintain Discipline** Focus is a discipline, just as working hard, and being more organized, and managing your time better, is. It is something at which you can get better. But focus is also very fragile. The tougher the times the more you have to focus. A leader is never more needed than during a crisis. During such times, your message must be that we will survive this. Your overall manner must be telling people that you are in control of the situation.

- **Avoid Distractions** Young people lose focus very quickly. They also have a difficult time envisioning the future. They are prone to distractions and changing interests, both of which cause them to lose focus on the task at hand. So anything you can do to minimize distractions is a plus. You must constantly be stressing fundamentals and the goals of the group.

- **Always Be Prepared** Being prepared is an essential part of being focused. The more prepared you are, the less chance you have of getting distracted. So much of success depends on preparation, on what you do before the actual event. Practice is not a luxury, not a penance. It's a key part of being focused.

GOLDA MEIR

Golda Meir is without question one of the most powerful and influential leaders of the twentieth century. At an age when most people have long since retired, she was elected Israel's prime minister, thus accepting the awesome responsibility of leading the youngest nation in one of the oldest and most troubled areas of the world—the Middle East.

Born in Russia, raised in Milwaukee, Golda Meir's life can be seen as one continuous struggle—first to create an independent Jewish state, then to protect the welfare and sovereignty of that state against a sea of hostile forces that sought to erase Israel from the map. Seldom in her life, from the time she first moved to Palestine in 1921 until her death in 1978, did she experience true and lasting peace. There were always obstacles to overcome and enemies to defeat.

To trace the arc of Golda Meir's life is to trace the history of Israel, from its birth to its rise as a powerful player on the world's stage. Lured by Zionist leader Theodor Herzl's dream of an independent homeland for the Jews, Golda Meir left the safety and security of life in the United States for an uncertain future in the turbulent, violent Middle East. She quickly distinguished herself as a strong advocate for her cause, and during the 1930s and 1940s she served in various Zionist organizations in Palestine, Europe, and the United States.

Then in 1948, following years of struggle, the dream of

Jews worldwide became a reality—the state of Israel was created. And Golda Meir was one of the signers of the proclamation insuring Israel's right to exist.

From there, Golda Meir served in a variety of capacities. In 1949, she was named minister of Labor and Social Insurance. She served as foreign minister from 1956 to '66. And from 1969 to '74, she held her country's highest position—prime minister. She was seventy years old when elected.

As a leader, Golda Meir was bold and uncompromising. She was simple, direct, and strong. Like her mentor, David Ben-Gurion (Israel's first prime minister), she was unyielding in her purpose and absolute in her convictions. If she wanted something, she was relentless in her efforts to make it happen. As labor minister, she fought a bitter battle against the Right to get more housing and better roads. In her role as foreign minister, and later as prime minister, she helped build up her country's military power by securing arms, weapons, and moral support from the U.S.

One of her greatest strengths as a leader was her ability to move an audience. Although she was tough, she could also be extremely compassionate. In virtually every area of concern, she put the human element first. But with a slight twist: While most leaders are moved by the pain of an individual and indifferent to the sufferings of the masses, she was the exact opposite. She wasn't easily swayed or impressed by individual appeals.

Throughout her political life, as the most prominent woman in a male-dominated world, Golda Meir was constantly challenged because of her gender. Her detractors charged her with being too emotional and swayed by feminine feelings rather than the cold logic necessary to successful leadership. But gender was a nonissue to her and she never allowed it to deter her from the task at hand.

Another of her great leadership attributes was her

simplicity of language. She was plainspoken, sometimes to the point of being rather blunt. Unlike those who wrap their words in countless layers of diplomatic mumbo-jumbo, Golda Meir aimed for clarity and truth. Her language was always a delicate fusion of warmth and toughness.

Golda Meir ruled her government with an iron hand. At home or in the office, she was always the boss. And yet, she was quick to elicit—and assess—the opinions of others before making her final decision. She absorbed the collective wisdom of her colleagues, constantly probing them to point out and challenge her own instincts. After hearing from all sides, and after weighing the available options, she acted in a quick, clear-minded manner.

If Golda Meir had a weakness, it was her inability to forgive and forget. She held grudges. If you wronged Israel—or her—she was incapable of showing mercy. The Arab refugee problem was the perfect example of this. She was adamant in her belief that Israel was not to blame for the plight of displaced Arabs, a situation she saw as the direct result of the Arabs' attempts to destroy Israel.

In typical, tough Golda Meir language, she said, "I am sorry; I cannot sympathize with the poor Arab states because they failed to exterminate us."

Like any leader, Golda Meir made mistakes. Her unyielding, unsympathetic attitude toward the Arabs only served to stir Palestinian pride while furthering resentment of the Israelis. It was this bitterness that led to the Yom Kippur War in 1973.

In the aftermath of that conflict, Golda Meir was severely criticized for not being more aware of Arab troop buildups. One year later, she resigned as Israeli prime minister.

Golda Meir died in Jerusalem in 1978.

* * *

Although her political career ended on a sour note, there can be no denying the important role Golda Meir played in the creation of Israel and its subsequent rise to world prominence. In many ways, she *was* Israel—tough, independent-minded, and headstrong in the pursuit of freedom and liberty. Golda Meir's spirit was as indomitable as the land for which she fought.

9

LIVE FOR THE FUTURE,
NOT IN THE PAST

When I came to the Celtics as head coach and president in the spring of 1997, I arrived with a vision. It was clear and direct. We wanted to be in the playoffs by the third or fourth year. We wanted to be a championship contender by the fifth or sixth year. That was the vision, our long-range plan. I was also becoming part of a franchise that had one of the most storied traditions in all of sports, sixteen world championships, including one stretch from the late fifties through the sixties when the Celtics won eleven world titles in thirteen years.

Yet it also was an organization that had grown stale. The Celtics were at the lowest point in their history. They had just concluded a season in which they only had won fifteen games and attendance was down. Larry Bird, Kevin McHale, and Robert Parish—the cornerstone of the great Celtics teams of the eighties —were all gone, and the cheers seemed to have left with them. The glory days seemed far away. The year before, the Celtics had moved into the new FleetCenter, adjacent to the old Boston Garden, but it seemed as if all the good memories were in the old Garden next door.

This was the reality I was walking into and there were many people who thought I should just come in and clean house, simply wipe the slate clean and begin all over again. Their reasoning was that the organization was in such dire straits that it needed a symbolic overhaul: out with the old, in with the new.

But the new job was a balancing act. If it was obvious that the Celtics needed a reorganization, the problem was what to do. I was very cognizant of the great tradition of the Celtic past, that this was like some precious heirloom that had to be treasured. I had to honor the past, but I had to upgrade, too. You can't live off tradition. That's one of the things I learned at Kentucky, where the first thing I had to do was clean up the mess that had put them on NCAA probation.

It's a fine line to walk as a leader. You must pay homage to the great tradition, because that's one of the things that makes you special, but you have to be future-oriented, too. The worst thing you can do is get bogged down in the past and rest on laurels that have long since withered. We can learn from the past, but we can't live in it.

BRIDGE THE GAP BETWEEN THE PAST AND THE FUTURE

Before I came to Boston, one of the first things I did in my negotiations with Celtic owner Paul Gaston was to insist that if anyone in the organization were to be let go, he had to do it, and he had to do it before I arrived. I was not going to be placed in a situation where the first thing I did as the new leader was to change people. All that would have done was make the people who didn't get fired extremely leery of me, so handling this prior to my coming aboard was essential.

While the organization has to take care of the past, a new leader has to take care of the future. Your message is about the future and how it's going to be better for everyone. Your message is this is the start of a new era. It's an uplifting message, one filled with hope and potential, and you don't want it clouded by having to fire people as your first official act. Change is difficult enough for people without your being perceived as the Grim Reaper.

Yes, we needed to resurrect the franchise, but many of the changes had to be subtle and gradual before a total transformation could take place. When I first came on board with the Celtics, I soon realized that the people remaining in the organization were very good at what they did; there wasn't any need for major change there. The marketing people, the promotional people, the business people—all these departments were operating well, so there was no reason to disrupt what they were doing.

An important key for leaders to help keep their eye on the future is to constantly be upgrading. This is the world of high technology. And just as the technology keeps changing, today's computer becoming virtually obsolete by next year, you must always be looking for ways to make the parts of an organization better. That's your game plan: short-term goals to manage the present, long-term goals for the future. And with your short-term goals your methods are going to change as the different obstacles appear before you.

For example, when I got the job in the spring of 1997, we figured that we would either get Tim Duncan or Keith Van Horn in the NBA draft. Since the Celtics had finished last in the league, we had the highest percentage of landing the first pick in the NBA draft lottery for my first season. Even if we didn't get the first pick—which everyone knew would be Duncan, then having ended a great career at Wake Forest—we expected at least the second pick, which everyone knew would be Van Horn. Either one of them would have dramatically upgraded our talent level and would have given us a jump start on our vision of being in the playoffs by the third year, and being a championship contender by the fifth year.

That didn't happen. By some mixture of fate and bad luck, we ended up with the third and sixth pick, which was a dramatic falloff. Would we be better now with either Duncan or Van Horn? No question. But that's where the importance of flexibility comes in: You can't feel sorry for yourself, just as you can't sit around and lament what might have been. You simply must keep upgrading as much as you can, whether it's with people, facilities, or technology. Your daily goals are to keep making things better, but your vision remains constant.

ACT, DON'T REACT

Poor leaders lack vision. They are too locked into the present tense, either bogged down in daily problems or simply reacting to past failures. They too often seem to bounce from crisis to crisis, always with an eye out for the next one around the corner. Their view of the future is hazy because they're always too concerned about the present. They are more concerned with managing than leading.

There's a difference between management and leadership: leaders lead; managers manage. Managers are the ones that oversee the rules and values of the organization. By definition, they function within the parameters of the organization and often, when faced with a situation outside of these parameters, they're not sure how to act.

Leaders are not hampered by such restrictions. It's their role to stretch the organization, change it. Leaders are the ones who provide the vision.

Take the bottom NBA teams, for example. In the past two decades it's always the same story: A so-called tough coach leaves only to be replaced by a so-called player's coach, only to have the cycle repeated over and over. The organization has waffled back and forth and when one coach leaves all the blemishes come out, leaving the new coach to always start at ground zero. The same repetitive cycle over and over again.

The problem with the Nets during this time was that there

was never any vision, never any grand plan that exceeded hiring some new coach who was the philosophical opposite of the one who just left. Instead of trying to actualize a grand plan to find the perfect leader for their team, they always were reacting to what had been tried before, forever a yo-yo.

Many companies are just like this. One CEO leaves, another takes his place, only to be replaced by still another somewhere down the line. Management styles come and management styles go; yet when you talk to people in the actual workplace nothing really changes at all, at least not substantively. It's all style, like constantly putting new paint on an old house. When all is said and done you still have the same old house. The same problems never really go away, they just get camouflaged for a while.

This is a common failing of leaders who don't have a vision. The result is they always seem to be reacting instead of acting, always trying to fix the mistakes of the past. If plan A fails, they try plan B. If B fails, they try plan A again, and on and on it goes back and forth. When one plan fails the leader tries another one, but all the plans are short-sighted, designed solely to deal with the present problem at hand. It's a little like trying to rake leaves in a windstorm: You can work very hard and have all the right intentions, but invariably you fail because you simply haven't planned very well.

Poor leaders never seem able to transcend the past. They are forever wallowing in it, caught in its quicksand. Instead of moving everyone toward a different future, they seem unable to escape past failures and their ramifications.

A leader's lack of vision also eventually cripples the people being led. Without a vision to inspire employees and see where their works fit into the big picture, all work eventually seems like a station on a bad assembly line, another numbing day at a boring task, with little understanding of where it can lead. Ultimately, it becomes work in all the negative aspects of the word and nothing more. People in these situations invariably begin working for themselves, their view of the future not extending beyond the next paycheck. These people have little loyalty and virtually no allegiance.

Why should they? They've been given no alternative. They become the kind of people that look at the highway and just see more highway, not where that highway can take them.

PUT YOUR TEAM IN "FUTURE THINK"

Shortly after I began coaching at Boston University, I learned that if I was going to put that carrot out there I had to tell my players where it was going to take them. I couldn't just keep making them work hard because I said so, because eventually they would start questioning what all the hard work was for. I had to have a vision and I had to be able to impart that vision to my team. A leader has to tell the people he is leading where the vision is going to take them.

Let's look at a failing company. The CEO is let go, another one comes in to take his place. What's he do? Often, the script plays out like this: The new CEO immediately lays off 20 percent of the workforce, leaving the remaining 80 percent filled with doubt and anxiety. Their morale is awful. They fear the future. Their way of dealing with this is to become focused on themselves.

What that CEO should do is the opposite. The first thing new leaders have to do is explain their vision. Then they have to locate the talent in the company. Immediately reducing the workplace before becoming familiar with the talent available will hurt your potential. Don't listen to hearsay. Determine it firsthand. The worst mistake you can make is to eliminate on other people's impressions people who could have helped you.

New leaders can't come into the workplace like a business version of some medieval chieftain, leaving bodies scattered in their wake. They can't come in and instantly change everything. New leaders have to come in promising hope, come in with a vision of the future that doesn't contradict the good aspects of the organization's past.

In his book *Think Like a Champion*, Denver Broncos' Mike Shanahan talks about one of this first coaching jobs, as an assistant at his alma mater, Eastern Illinois.

"There was some talk that the school was going to drop its football program, particularly since it hadn't had a winning season in seventeen years," Shanahan writes. "Twenty-one of the twenty-two players from the team that had finished 1-10 the previous season were returning for the next season. They were the laughingstock of the state. But why let the past determine the future? With an expanded coaching role for me and with new leadership in place—Eastern Illinois had hired former University of Arizona and Florida State head coach Darrell Mudra, who, for good reason, was nicknamed 'Dr. Victory'—it was time to believe anything was possible.

"'Men,' he told our players and coaching staff, 'you are going to be winners. I've looked at a lot of film and know the talent we have and I know we will get to the (Division II) playoffs with the right plan and the right attitude. There is no reason why we can't win a national championship.'

"Everyone looked at him as if he was high on drugs, including me. I thought we definitely could win, but he was talking about a national championship when we hadn't had a winning record in nearly twenty years. But in the end of the season, he was right. . . . We won the national championship. . . . And now that I look back on it I shouldn't have been surprised at all. Coach Mudra had a vision and he would not be denied."

Shanahan's story is a classic example of vision.

As we talked about in the first chapter, establishing the vision from the beginning is essential, because it makes you immediately deal with the future. It moves the focus away from the past. It makes everyone start to look forward instead of behind. It establishes the dream and that's the environment you are trying to create: everyone pursuing the dream of a better future.

SELL POSSIBILITY

Creative people are valuable to any group. They are innovative and have many ways to make things better. But being creative doesn't necessarily mean that they know how to execute those ideas. And execution is the key. How do you get your product out there? How do you get people to be aware of your message? How do you get people to believe in you? How do you deliver? How do you win?

These are the questions that will determine whether you ultimately succeed or fail. Execution is what victories are made of.

If you believe in some new idea or strategy, you have to market that belief and sell it. Sell it to your management team. Sell it to your employees. Sell it to the world that's watching you. And you do this by the step-by-step execution of your game plan into a real-life program. What you are looking for is a greater percentage of the marketplace. But you must market your program to everyone. Nothing is more significant than this. Every person involved is important, because you are trying to sell them all. You market your message to everyone and hope you get your percentage. That's why when I'm out in public I never mind signing autographs. My job is to create more Celtics fans, so everywhere I go I market the Boston Celtics.

Why do I do this? Why is this important when the Celtics are as much a Boston institution as the Freedom Trail and the Old North Church?

I know how important a constant marketing program is because I personally witnessed the Yankees and Kentucky basketball floundering and saw them go through their bad times, these two sports giants that no one thought could flounder. We are in a very competitive business, where not everyone can be successful. If the Roman Empire can fall, the Boston Celtics certainly can fall.

In the fall of 1999, following the NBA lockout, we were

down one thousand season tickets from the year before at the same time. So I wrote a letter to every season ticket owner who did not reapply. My message to them?

"I don't blame you. I wouldn't renew either. Last year's team didn't play with Celtic Pride. But . . . "

Then I listed how the upcoming year was going to be different. How we had learned from the year before, that there was going to be a significant turnaround and they were not going to want to miss it.

The letter was successful. It was simple, it was low cost, and it addressed the issue of concern to fans.

For the same reason the FleetCenter had a cruise for season ticket holders, as well as parties for season ticket holders and parties for sponsors. Our strategy is to bring the Celtics to people, for we must keep the Celtics out there in the public eye. In a sense we're competing with the Red Sox, the Patriots, the Bruins. We're competing with the movies and videos. It's all the entertainment dollar and we are trying to maintain our percentage.

We can't take anything for granted. We must keep looking to create new fans—more season ticket holders—to increase our fan base. They are the future. Without them, we won't have a future.

MARKET TO YOUR FUTURE

There is a book called *The Servant As Leader* by Robert K. Greenleaf, and its contention is that in today's business climate everything must be geared to the customer and to the people who service those customers. This idea has reached a point where in some companies now it's the customers who get the prized parking spot, not the CEO or the executives. The premise is that leaders have to be servants because the key people are 1) the customers, and 2) the people who service the customers' needs.

That book is right on target. Look at many of the large food chains, the ones that deal in volume. Their profit margin on what they sell is so slim that they need a steady flow of customers. They can't afford to take their success for granted. They can't afford to get complacent. They must continue to deal in volume. They must continue to generate new customers, as well as keeping the ones they have satisfied. So even with all their success there is always pressure to keep marketing their product, keep adding new customers.

There's a lesson there for anyone who is leading an organization. In January of 1999, shortly after the NBA lockout ended, the Celtics traveled to Providence, Rhode Island, and Worcester, Massachusetts, to hold a free workout for the public. It was our way of trying to win the fans back, our version of the olive branch. In both places we had the players greeting the fans as they entered the building, plus signing autographs.

I did this, too. In Providence, I was asked by a sports writer why I continued to stand in the lobby signing autographs until all the people were gone.

"Because they're our customers," I answered. "And you don't shut the door on customers and tell them the door's closed. All the people I was signing autographs for were either customers or potential customers."

A good example of this is 76ers owner Pat Croce, who stands outside and greets people as they walk into the arena. Here is someone who understands public relations, and that people will leave the arena feeling good about the 76ers, and the way thet were treated.

The real question is: Why did it take a lockout for us in the NBA to realize this? Why didn't we realize that professional sports, like any other business, is about marketing?

Take the Celtics, for example. Back in the eighties, when they had Larry Bird, they really didn't have to market themselves. They were one of the elite teams in the game. They sold out every night. Who needed marketing? But we don't have Larry Bird anymore. We have a new building with roughly six thousand more seats than the old Boston Garden and we have to market our product. It's not enough just to announce the schedule and wait for the people to flock into the building the way it was done in the Bird era. It's all in the marketing of the team to keep us focused on what will work in the future, not on what worked in the past.

It's a lesson I learned at Boston University.

When I got that job in 1977 they were probably drawing fifty to seventy-five people a game, so our plan was to do whatever it took to get more people to come to the games. I visited dormitories. We had raffles. We passed out pamphlets.

The first year I decided to do a "Midnight Madness" party, to celebrate the start of our first practice at the stroke of midnight on October 15th, the first day you're allowed to practice. Lefty Dreisell had originated the idea a few years earlier at Maryland, and I thought it would be a great way to generate some interest. Our plan was to get a lot of people, have champagne toasts, and introduce everyone to the new era that was beginning at Boston University. That was the plan, anyway, and we were psyched. We passed out pamphlets. We spread the word around. We expected between five hundred and a thousand people. We even had about thirty bottles of champagne. This was going to be the start of something special.

Thirty-six people showed up.

Sixteen were family and close friends. Another ten were our boosters. And the other ten? Guys with a strong affinity for alcohol who cared very little about basketball. Guys who had wandered in searching for the free champagne. I was crushed.

What was I going to tell my team who were in the locker room thinking they were about to run out before a cheering crowd? What were we going to do with all the champagne?

In the beginning, nothing seemed to make any difference at BU. I would speak at dormitories that had maybe a thousand kids in them and six would show up to hear me speak. We would pass out thousands of pamphlets and get a dozen extra people to a game. We would ask ourselves, Why? What were we doing wrong? We told ourselves our potential fans were out there; we just weren't reaching them.

I was told not to worry about it, that BU was an apathetic campus, that there were just too many other things to do than go to a college basketball game to see a team that hadn't had a winning season since anyone could remember.

But I wasn't satisfied with this attitude. I wanted to see this program have a promising future, not be saddled with the indifference of the past years. So I began to learn what customers are all about.

We had to identify a BU fan, to try and get a good solid core of seven hundred people who would come and support us. That became our aggressive goal, and even though they still left us with about thirteen hundred empty seats, we couldn't worry about that. We had to respect the seven hundred people who were there. We had to make sure they kept coming back. That was our job. Respect the seven hundred who were coming, while all the time trying to add to that number. That became the goal. Eventually, we got to fifteen hundred people. But it took four years.

In retrospect, I know this is where I developed my philosophy of marketing. If you keep selling your product and don't take anything for granted, you can transform an organization even when the odds say you can't.

Just because you've been successful in the past is no guarantee of anything in the future. No matter what your résumé says, you can very quickly demolish the past, whether at an organizational level or an individual one. We can all name countless once-successful companies that have fallen off the earth, companies that once were thought to be untouchable. When I was a kid every serious basketball player wore Converse sneakers. Everybody. They dominated the marketplace. Now? They're fighting to survive in an industry where it often seems that Nike rules the world.

The point is that all companies are fragile, even the so-called giants. There is so much competition. Individual trends and fashions are constantly in motion. The marketplace is always changing. It's hard enough to get to the top, but it's harder to stay there. The talent is so close, the difference between winning and losing is so thin. Things can change in a heartbeat. Yes, we have a national championship at Kentucky. Yes, we went to three Final Fours in five years. Yes, we won in the pros with the Knicks.

But it's all meaningless as far as how I'm judged today.

If I don't win with the Celtics, none of these accomplishments will be anything other than nice items on a biography page. In today's culture, we're all being judged on how we do now. Coaches always have known that. The realities of their profession convince us very early that the past is for scrapbooks, that if you are not successful it doesn't matter what your résumé says, you will be let go.

That's the way it is today in business also. You're a new CEO and you have a five-year plan? Well, your stockholders want to see results now. They want to make money now. If there's no success in two years, odds are that CEO won't be around in that fifth year.

We live in a very impatient society. Intellectually, people understand that rebuilding takes time. Emotionally? They don't have the patience for it. So you must always trying to make the future arrive sooner.

LOOK FOR LEADERS AROUND YOU

One of the great models for any organization is a professional football team. Football is the sport which most closely mirrors a company. In football, more than any other sport, there is a definite chain of command. There is the head coach. Then there is an offensive coordinator and a defensive coordinator and the respective coaches who work underneath both. So the head coach is not so much coaching the players as he is coaching the other coaches. He imparts his daily vision to his assistant coaches. They, in turn, impart it to the players.

This is the blueprint that most companies follow. It is also the model I follow, both as the president of the Celtics and as the coach. I rely on others to help us become more successful.

Jim O'Brien, who was with me when I coached the Knicks and also at Kentucky, is in charge of the defense and how the other team plays. He breaks down the other team's film, formulates a game plan on how to play them. Lester Connor, another assistant, is in charge of the offense.

After each game, we break down the film and grade everything. How we fought over screens. How many loose balls we got. How many deflections we got. How many rebounds. Where our shots came from. Everything is broken down; everything graded. We do this on both offense and defense. There is nothing left to memory, nothing left to interpretation.

Then we show it to the players. Seeing it on film is powerful. It allows the coaches not to be endlessly harping on the transgressions, something which has the potential to be resented by the players. Instead, the players can see it for themselves.

We also have two video people who help the team. Let's say we're going to play Portland, for example. One person would be responsible for putting together a video on Scottie Pippen. It would show where he scores from. What side does he usually go on the floor? Where does his shot come from? What side does he like to post up on? The point is to tell the people who are likely to guard Pippen all his tendencies, although we only will give the players about 50 percent of the information we get, because we want them to be able to assimilate what we give them, not be overloaded with it.

But it is not enough just to have your staff on board.

Ever since I came to the Celtics in May of 1997 I have been looking for some players who are going to become leaders. If you look at all great athletic teams, one of the constants is good veteran leadership. From the great Celtics teams of the eighties with Larry Bird, to the Lakers of the same era, to the Chicago Bulls with Michael Jordan, a common thread running through these teams was the presence of great leadership on the court. Bird, Magic, and Jordan were not just great basketball players. They were great leaders as well—to the point that if teammates did not work hard in practice *they* would get on them, not just the coach. In a sense, these teams didn't really need a strong leader as the coach, for the coach's principles and strategies were constantly being reinforced by these great players. This is the perfect scenario.

For I know that my voice can't always be the only voice they hear. That simply won't work over the long haul. Eventually, that one voice will get tuned out, like so much loud music that you can't wait to turn the volume down on. So my message must be constantly reinforced by others.

In my first season in 1997–'98 I knew that my voice was not there the minute I left the locker room. The players were either too young or didn't possess proper leadership traits to continue my voice—my message—when I wasn't physically there.

That's why I signed Popeye Jones at the start of my second year, the shortened season in 1999. He is old by NBA standards and was coming off injuries, so I knew it would be a period of time before he would be able to regain his physical skills. But I know his leadership skills hadn't disappeared. He is a voice of experience, someone who not only has been through the NBA wars, but has a perspective on them. With Popeye I knew I didn't always have to be physically present for my message to be heard. So I was paying him more for his leadership than for his talent and that leadership is something the Celtics so desperately need.

That leadership is something I need.

And even if I eventually traded Popeye to Denver in the summer of 1999, as part of the deal that sent Ron Mercer to the Nuggets for Danny Fortson and Eric Williams, I always appreciated Popeye's veteran leadership.

In my first year with the Celtics, the 1997–'98 season, I made Pervis Ellison a captain. Pervis is a veteran whose career had been hampered by injuries and the perception was that he doesn't want it enough, that he's content to do the minimum and coast. He is virtually a poster child for this perception, even though in many ways he's a delightful man. So I named him captain as a motivational tool, hoping that the honor would make him play through his nagging injuries and begin to reach his full potential.

Unfortunately, Popeye experienced further injuries and never had a chance to showcase his leadership abilities. But I still believe that this is a useful tool to help determine who's got what it takes to be a future leader.

I also named Antoine Walker as another captain. He is our best player, one of the most talented young players in the NBA, someone who I recruited out of high school and someone who played two years for me at Kentucky. Now Antoine is a great talent. He had come to Kentucky from Chicago where he was a talented high school player who was creative with the ball, the kind of player who never met a shot he didn't like. That never bothered me at the time, because a lot of great high school players think shot first. I recruited him because he was a great competitor, was an extremely versatile player, and because his first college choice had been to come to Kentucky.

When I coached him at Kentucky my task was to make him more team-oriented, while not inhibiting either his talent or his competitiveness. It's a delicate balance. You want him to think "team" first, but you also don't want to put too many reins on his talent. It's a little like having a great salesman whose personality tends to turn off many people in the office. You want him to soften his personality for the sake of the group, but you also don't want him to lose that certain swagger that makes him such a good salesman.

So whenever Antoine used his excellent passing skills while at Kentucky and began playing less selfishly, I publicly pointed this out. Whenever I had the chance I would publicly acknowledge Antoine's willingness to become more team-oriented at the expense of his individual stats as one of the keys to our success. At the large press conference on the day before the national semifinals in the Meadowlands in New Jersey—with Antoine being one of the players with me at the press conference—I again stressed that Antoine's transformation as a player was one of the reasons why we had been so successful, for what you have to do with young people is constantly reinforce the kind of behavior for which you're striving. You can't take it for granted. You can't let it go unnoticed. You have to acknowledge it as much as you can.

Antoine left Kentucky after his sophomore year to enter the NBA draft. It was the year we won the national title, and Antoine parlayed that and his great potential to become the sixth pick in the draft.

His first year with the Celtics he had been one of the impact rookies in the league, a future star in the making. When I began coaching him with the Celtics it was quickly apparent to me that Antoine was still much like what he'd been in his two years in Kentucky—very talented, but still immature as a player. I was hoping that making Antoine a captain would escalate the maturation process, make Antoine be more of a leader. It's what the Seattle SuperSonics did with Gary Payton, another extremely talented young player with a reputation for being extremely volatile. The Sonics were publicly asking Payton to mature, and he did, to a point.

But I have learned that before you can change someone you must build a trust. My message to Antoine going into the 1999–2000 season was that, even though he might read things in the newspaper attributed to me that he might not like, the reality is that I recruited him to Kentucky, we won a national championship at Kentucky together, and I gave him a contract worth $12 million a year. So that the reality is Rick Pitino is behind Antoine Walker, and that Antoine Walker has to be behind Rick Pitino; that we've already had some great times together and now we have to have great times with the Celtics together. What I'm trying to do with Antoine is to convince him that we need each other.

So far, the jury is still out, but I still believe in his talent and his ability to be loyal to the organization.

I also have learned that as a leader I must delegate. I have to trust the people I have working for me. I have to believe in *their* leadership abilities and I must institute a system of checks and balances to make sure they can be as successful as possible. By showing confidence in others, I am placing a bet on their abilities and how they contribute to our organization in the future, rather than limiting their role to how they've performed in the past.

Where is your group going to be down the road?

What are your people going to be down the road?

Can you get them to reach their potential and if you can, how long is that going to take?

The mistake many people make is they give up on people too soon. They either can't see the potential or they feel they can't afford to wait for it.

But it's a fine line. It's the problem I have with Antoine Walker heading into the 1999–2000 season. Yes, he's a great talent. Someday he's going to mature. But is someday going to be your day? That's the tricky question. His true greatness as an NBA player will probably come in his seventh or eighth year as a pro. But will I be there then?

That's the question you eventually have to answer: Are you going to stay the course or are you going to change? Is it failure or just adversity? You are the captain of the ship and you have to decide whether it's a storm or just choppy seas. But you have to sur-round yourself with creative people and you must build alliances with them.

DON'T SURROUND YOURSELF
WITH "YES" MEN

The people who work for you must be dependable and trustwor-thy. Hopefully, you will be able to depend on them during diffi-cult times. But they must be creative, too. You must allow people around you to express themselves. You don't want "yes" men, people who are always going to tell you want you want to hear. They must be able to tell you when they think you're wrong.

I learned this from Hubie Brown, whom I worked for two years with the New York Knicks in the early eighties. I was amazed at how much teaching he allowed me to do. He always allowed me to express myself. He listened to my ideas. He let me have great input in practice. He sought my advice during games. His main objective as a leader was to make things better, not to be unquestioned. That's an important distinction. Leaders who are not secure in their role don't want their authority questioned. Leaders who are secure always want to make things better, what-ever it takes.

The more responsibility you give your lieutenants the stronger you make them. And the stronger they are the stronger you are.

If you watched us practice with the Celtics you would see that all my assistant coaches have a role. There's no question I'm in charge, but everyone has their job to do. They all have their own areas of responsibility. I want their input, their ideas. I want them to make decisions and I also want their feedback. I not only want it, I need it.

You must be willing to be evaluated by people for without

constant feedback, you can't be a great leader. When I'm in staff meetings I am forever asking my staff what they think about things, constantly challenging them for more feedback. Otherwise, it's like living inside a hothouse, unrealistically sheltered from all cold, hard facts of the world. The more observations and insight you get from the people around you, the better able you are to make better decisions.

You must be able to listen. As a young coach I didn't do that very well. In retrospect, I'm sure some of my assistants were afraid to question me, convinced I wouldn't handle their feedback very well, that I would snap at them. They were probably too intimidated to challenge me and that was my failing. But I couldn't coach that way now, even if I wanted to. It simply wouldn't work. I have come to learn that the more feedback the better.

If I can get one or two things from the variety of books I read, then reading that book helped me. That's really all I'm looking for, one or two things. The more things you learn from the people around you, the better you're able to execute.

I also want feedback from my players. I want to know what bothers them, what makes them go sideways. I want to know as much about them as possible. Their moods, their frustrations, their hopes and dreams. I want to know what they want, what they expect. In short, I am in search of the truth. And the only way you start to get as close to that as you possibly can is to receive as much information as possible.

What I'm also in search of is providing the environment in which potential can flourish. That's always your bottom line. As a leader, you're always looking toward the future, an environment where the past is buried and present-day problems are solved in ways that do not get in the way of your long-term goals. You have to stick close to your vision of where you're going. That's the beacon you always are moving toward and you must never lose sight of it.

KEY CHAPTER POINTS

● **Bridge the Gap Between the Past and the Future** You must respect an organization's histories and traditions, but you always must be upgrading, too. The key is to always be making it better. Your game plan is short-term goals to manage the present; long-term goals for the future. The emphasis, though, always has to be on the future.

● **Act, Don't React** Poor leaders lack vision. They are too locked into the present tense, endlessly being bogged down by either daily problems or past failures. This is not acting, this is reacting. Leaders act. You must forever be using people toward the future.

● **Put Your Team in "Future Think"** You can never let people lose sight of your vision, what you're trying to accomplish as an organization and where you're trying to go. This is the flag you always have to be waving, even during those times when everyone seems immersed in the present tense.

● **Sell Possibility** You always have to be selling the future. You can't be satisfied with what you've already accomplished, you always have to be pushing forward, making people aware of the possibilities.

● **Market to Your Future** You also always have to be selling your product, no matter how successful it is. You can't take anything for granted. You must understand that all organizations are fragile and that today's success can instantly become tomorrow's failure.

● **Look for Leaders Around You** You must always be looking for future leaders, the ones who are going to spread your message. You can't be the only voice people hear. You must surround yourself with creative people and build alliances with them.

● **Don't Surround Yourself with "Yes" Men** You need feedback from people. You need to create an environment where creativity can flourish. Surrounding yourself with people who are afraid to tell you what they feel—for whatever reason—gets in the way of this.

ST. IGNATIUS LOYOLA

St. Ignatius Loyola, founder of the Society of Jesus (Jesuits), seems to have been one of those rare human beings born with a natural instinct for leadership. Throughout his remarkable life, whether on the field of battle or in service to his God, Ignatius consistently demonstrated the many skills that make a successful leader. He could be tough, fearless, loving, dogged in his determination, and kind.

Above all else, St. Ignatius was admired and respected by friends and foes alike.

The arc of Ignatius's life is as remarkable as the man himself. Few men in history have ended so far from where they began. Until he was in his early thirties, Ignatius was as far removed from the spiritual world as he could possibly have been. And it was only by chance that he ended up following a far different path.

Ignatius was born in 1491, the youngest of thirteen children in the Basque province of Guipúzcoa in northern Spain. As a young man, he was something of a scoundrel. Gambling, drinking, chasing women, fighting—those were young Ignatius's primary endeavors. At one point, following an altercation, Ignatius was forced to flee his town. He was eventually brought back and made to stand trial, but thanks to the influence of higher-ups, the case against him was dropped.

It was through violence that Ignatius became a man of love. At age thirty, as an officer defending the town of Pamplona from the French, Ignatius was severely wounded in both legs when struck by a cannonball. Although the injuries eventually healed, surgery left one leg shorter than the other, causing him to walk with a limp for the remainder of his life.

While recuperating, Ignatius asked for something to read. He wanted romance novels, but instead was given a copy of the life of Christ and a book on the saints. Reading those books was the beginning of his spiritual journey.

He made his confession at a Benedictine shrine, then spent the next ten months living alone in a cave, praying, contemplating, and shaping the ideas that became known as the Spiritual Exercises. Later, while standing on the banks of a river, Ignatius had a vision, one that revealed to him that God can be found in all things.

At thirty-three, now determined to study for the priesthood, Ignatius returned to school. It was while studying at the university that Ignatius's zeal—and his somewhat unorthodox beliefs—brought him to the attention of the Spanish Inquisition and landed him in jail for forty-two days. He was released but was viewed with such skepticism by certain Dominicans that he was only allowed to teach the simplest religious truths to children.

This unwillingness to conform to the most traditional Catholic beliefs often got Ignatius in hot water with his superiors. For instance, after founding the Jesuits, Ignatius never set fixed times or duration for prayers. It was his belief that if God can be found in all things, then all times are times of prayer. This, of course, was seen as heresy by many Catholic leaders and was one of the reasons why many were opposed to the formation of the Society of Jesus.

Formal approval for the Society of Jesus was granted by Pope Paul III on September 27, 1540. Initially, there were eight members and they unanimously elected Ignatius to be the group's superior. Ignatius would spend the remainder of his life overseeing the growth and expansion of the Jesuit order. By the time of his death in 1556, the number of Jesuits had swelled from eight to more than a thousand and they had opened schools in such distant places as Germany, India, Italy, and the Netherlands. Ignatius directed this growth from two small rooms that served as his living quarters and his office.

What kind of leader was Ignatius? Well, for one thing, as we've already seen, he wasn't afraid to march to the beat of a different drummer. By discarding the notion that an individual's destiny was carved in stone, arguing instead that each person could, through religious zeal and extended spiritual searching, attain a state of enlightenment, he challenged the entrenched beliefs of the Catholic Church.

Ignatius was also a great believer in communicating with those within the order. During his fifteen years as superior general of the Jesuits, he wrote more than seven thousand letters. Unity of purpose and vision was seen by Ignatius as vital to the success of the Jesuits and their goals.

He was a stringent believer in putting the good of the group ahead of an individual's desire for glory or success. In this way, Ignatius was reverting to his old military philosophy. Without a doubt, Ignatius would have been a successful coach, because his approach, that of getting each individual player to sacrifice personal glory for the good of the team, is at the very heart of coaching. Ignatius was able to do that and that's leadership.

Ignatius was never a thinker on a grand scale. Instead, he had a singleness of purpose and an extraordinary eye for detail. He was known to rewrite letters up to twenty times, crafting them over and over until he was satisfied that his message was as close to perfect as possible.

Like most great leaders, Ignatius could be confusing and paradoxical. Although he was famous for being kind and loving toward those who gave him problems, he could, on occasion, be excessively harsh and demanding toward those who were holy and humble. Also, he could be sarcastic or biting in his re-marks. But in the end, one of his greatest strengths as a leader was that he treated all people equally, with respect and dignity, and as individuals. He didn't differentiate, and he never labeled people as friends or foes. He loved them all equally.

* * *

Ignatius, the former scoundrel and soldier, was beatified in 1609 and later canonized by Pope Gregory XV on March 12, 1622.

10

ACT SELFLESSLY

Leading the Celtics has been, without question, the most difficult challenge I've ever had in my professional life.

Acquiring and keeping talent with the NBA's salary cap is extremely difficult, as is coaching contemporary athletes. I can't always understand why it's so difficult to reach today's players, and after talking to a variety of coaches in the NBA, the problem is not endemic to just the Boston Celtics.

But I can't sit back, throw up my hands, and say, "Well, this is the culture," and do nothing about it. I must find a way to reach them.

In the 1999–2000 season it wasn't until we had a trip right after Christmas that I saw a glimmer of hope. We left Christmas night for Los Angeles to play the Clippers, a game we thought was winnable if we played the right way. The point I tried to make to the team was that the Clippers were going to take a lot of three-point shots, even if these shots were challenged. We had to limit their three-point shot attempts and force them to drive to the basket. Sure enough, when it looked like we were in control of the game, the Clippers started taking three-point shots and making them. The result was we lost a hard-fought game.

Afterward, we were all down. Everything we said had come true.

Then we proceeded on to Sacramento.

The Kings pass the ball very well. They have great ball movement and great player movement. In short, they have great teamwork and we lost another hard-fought game, Sacramento eventually pulling away in the fourth quarter.

Next, we headed to Denver.

On paper, this was the most difficult game of the trip. Not only are the Nuggets very tough at home, but we had had a big trade with Denver over the summer, so it promised to be an emotional game, too. Plus, we had blown them out three weeks earlier in the FleetCenter and they no doubt wanted revenge.

The day before the game we had a practice and for the first time all year I sensed a real malaise. We had a couple of guys faking injuries to get out of practice, to the point that we had to scrimmage four against four, and you could just sense that everyone was down, discouraged.

I was extremely upset.

The next morning I called the team together. I had stayed up most of the night thinking of some way to get them back, to get them to refocus.

I started off by telling them I knew it was a difficult road trip and I knew everyone was discouraged. I told them adversity was setting in and it was affecting everyone. I also told them I didn't like the way they were always "trash-talking" in practice, putting one another down, that I thought there was a danger in that, even though it was supposed to be in fun. Even though I was from another generation I told them I wouldn't try to change them unless I saw that their attitudes were contributing to a defeatist attitude.

Then I said that this was going to be the most important game they were going to play. That they had to prepare in everything they did and that they not only had to believe in the team, but in themselves, too. And that, "If you quit on yourself you have nothing left."

All of the players got juiced up.

Danny Fortson, who had played in Denver the year before, called them together and said that we were not going to lose. That night in the locker room you could see a dramatic change in attitude and it carried over into a great road victory for us.

The message?

Sometimes you have to first get people to believe in themselves. Then you get them to believe in the group.

Unfortunately, a few days later we went to New York and reverted back to all our bad habits.

But what we're looking for is improvement. Sixty percent is better than 40 percent. It's not as good as 80 percent, but it's better than 40.

What we're looking for is consistent growth. It's not always going to come as quickly as we want, and it's not going to be without its setbacks, but that's what we're always seeking.

We cannot let ourselves get ground down by failure. We must totally believe—and be very positive about—the future. That is what we're trying to do at the Celtics, even though we haven't been as successful as quickly as I had hoped. We are still struggling, still climbing, still scratching, and it's very easy to get down.

This is why I adopted my "98–2" philosophy at the start of the 1999–2000 season, my promise that I was going to try to always be 98 percent positive, even during the most trying of times.

I refuse to succumb to failure and one of the ways I do that is by looking at the travails of other leaders. Look at Joe Torre's career, for example. He managed the Braves, Mets, and Cardinals before he ever got the chance to manage the Yankees, and by his own admission he had come to view himself as someone who probably never was going to get a chance to win a championship. Dick Vermeil was viewed as being burned out as an NFL coach, someone who belonged to the past, before his St. Louis Rams came out of nowhere to win the Super Bowl in January of 2000. Bill Parcells, who is generally recognized as a Hall of Fame football coach, had a disappointing season with the Jets in 1999, primarily because his quarterback, Vinny Testaverde, got hurt in the first game and missed the rest of the season.

The lesson?

No leader has it easy all the time. There are always going to be rough stretches, down times, and you can't lose sight of that. It's all part of the learning experience of being a leader.

In mid-December 1999 we got beat at San Antonio and I felt about as low as I could be. I was exhausted, both mentally and physically. I was totally depressed. In truth, I felt very sorry for myself.

But you can't let failure keep you down. Failure is not the end of the world.

And it's all right to feel sorry for yourself once in a while. It's all right to have a bad day. It's all right to cry.

But then what are you going to do about it?

What you're going to do is get a good night's sleep and get up the next day ready to start fighting again.

That's what leaders do. They keep moving forward.

As a young coach I was more interested in personal accomplishments.

I think this is normal.

You are just starting out in your chosen career and you're trying to prove yourself. You tend to see the world in terms of "I." Your focus tends to be on your own goals, your own ambitions, your own successes, your own world. Certainly this was the case with me.

There are many times now when I lie awake at night and I can't fathom why my players do some of the things they do, think some of the things they think. Then I go back to the early days of my career and I understand. It's youth. And I understand the ills of being young. I had great passion, a great love for what I did, and without question I was trying to show people how good I was.

Never mind history repeating itself. People repeat themselves.

This is something all young people go through. In a sense I almost had tunnel vision back then. I was so consumed with mastering my craft, getting better at it, advancing my career, exulting with the wins, dying with the losses, absorbed in each individual season, that I failed to see the true test of leadership.

Once you get a little older, though, and you attain a certain measure of individual success, you start to realize that the only true success is group success; that true greatness is the ability to make those around you better.

This usually doesn't come in some great epiphany, one magic moment of sheer insight when you realize the error of your ways. Instead, it's usually a gradual process, evolving over time, until one day there it is in front of you as clear as day.

In basketball, this is what made Larry Bird and Magic Johnson such great players. It wasn't that they simply had great ability or were marvelous talents. Those were the obvious things, the qualities everyone could see. More subtle was their ability to raise the level of everyone else's play, too, their ability to always make their teammates better. That's what made them the icons of basketball they became. It's the lesson Michael Jordan had to learn when he first came into the NBA as a young player. Yes, he was an amazing talent from his first season. Yes, from the beginning it was apparent Michael had the kind of physical gifts for the game that one day were going to take him to the Hall of Fame. But it wasn't until he began understanding that he also had to make those around him better, too, that he began to win championships. It wasn't until he learned that he was an even greater player when he helped those around him succeed that he became the kind of mythic player we all remember.

In the book *Playing for Keeps*, David Halberstam writes

about how in the first years of his career in the NBA Jordan always was very tough on his teammates. He was such a perfectionist that he had little tolerance for people who didn't perform well or to the level he expected them to. It wasn't until he retired from basketball the first time and became a minor league baseball player that he changed. One theory is that because he struggled in baseball with his hitting he had more tolerance for failure when he came back to the Chicago Bulls. Whatever, after his baseball experience, Michael Jordan was a much more supportive teammate, an even better leader than he'd been before, more concerned with trying to make his teammates better.

That's a lesson we all can learn.

To be a great leader is to make everyone better. That's the greatest gift of all. To elevate the people around you, to get them to maximize their potential, to get them to reach their dreams. This is what the great leaders of history have done and it's what the great leaders do who are far from the spotlight, whether they are teachers, business leaders, or simply people leading a small group: They make the people around them succeed.

For, ultimately, leaders are judged by the success of the people they lead.

How you get them to be successful is not the issue, as there are almost as many leadership styles as there are leaders. The important thing is getting the people you lead to be successful.

This is the lesson I have finally learned after being a coach for over two decades, the one that transcends all the others.

My two years as the coach of the New York Knicks in the late eighties taught me that I wasn't going to out-coach anybody. The NBA was full of great coaches who worked hard and were very well prepared. The NBA was also full of great players, to the point that sometimes you could have the best game plan in the world and execute it flawlessly; you could do everything in your power as a coach to be prepared and still you would lose because sometimes great players are going to beat you regardless of what you do as a coach.

So I learned that the only thing that mattered as far as coaching was winning. Not how I coached. Not how I was perceived by the media or by the fans. None of that mattered anymore. Only winning. So my goal was to become the most successful coach I could be. To do that, I had to find a way to have my players be as successful as they could be.

That is what motivated me then and it's what motivates me to this day. The more I stay in coaching the more I know this is true.

The other thing I have come to know is that leaders must be selfless. It can't be just about you. Your career, your record. Your advancement, your success. Your dreams. It must be totally about the group.

Just as groups must be selfless.

That's why, as far as the other part of my job with the Celtics goes, I believe that the community involvement we do with the Celtics is very important. It's another way we can be selfless, reinforce the notion that the Boston Celtics are not just a professional basketball team, but an organization that's deeply imbedded in the community. So we give tickets to inner-city schoolkids for every home game. We support a variety of charities. We have community programs.

One of the things I instituted with the Celtics is something we call Heroes Among Us. Just as the Knicks and the Lakers make a big deal about the celebrities who sit in a special row at their home games, adding to the event, I felt we really needed something special at out home games in the FleetCenter, something that wasn't about Hollywood, but reflected Boston and the surrounding area. We are the medical and academic leader of the country and we wanted to do something to reflect that.

We came up with the ideas of honoring people in the community who are doing something significant, usually with little fanfare. These people come from all walks of life, the only common denominator being that they're doing something that makes life better, the real unknown heroes. So we announce them during the game and bring them to center court.

In addition to honoring worthy people, this also shows that the Boston Celtics are a vibrant part of the community. We live here. We work here. We are a part of the city's fabric. We not only recognize our roots in the community, we try to do significant things in the community whether it's giving to charities, having our players appear at schools and recreation centers, or giving away tickets to inner-city groups.

Hopefully, this also gives our employees a certain pride. Our message to them is we're not just a professional basketball team whose sole objective is to win games. We are the Boston Celtics, with one of the best traditions in all of sports, a franchise that's as much a part of the city of Boston as Faneuil Hall and the harbor, a franchise whose roots run deep, imbedded in the community. The Boston Celtics are special and to work for them is also special, but we also have to give back to the community that's supporting us. This is the message I want all our employees to have, from our players to our support people.

This is a message that can't be given enough, for it's at the heart of everything you're trying to do in building a group: get them to care about one another; get them to subordinate their self-interest to the goals of the group; get them to elevate the others around them.

OWN UP TO YOUR FLAWS

Many people think it's enough simply to be good at what you do. They work hard, they are constantly striving to make themselves better in their chosen profession, they do all the things they need to ensure their success. They think they're doing everything they have to do as the head of a company.

So when things don't go well they complain about their employees. Their assistants are either not good enough or they don't work hard enough, or both. The rank and file is lazy, only care about their paychecks and how quickly they can leave work. The younger people in the company seem to come from some other planet, almost as if they're some new form of mutation. Blah, blah, blah. We've all heard the litany. We've all probably used it ourselves at some point. It's human nature. We are working hard, yet something in the company seems to be missing. And we're not quite sure what to do about it, right?

Wrong.

You have fallen into a common trap. And it's a very simple one.

You have your vision, but it's strictly a personal one. You have your vision, but you aren't able to transform it to others. And if you cannot do that, then your vision will never get actualized, will simply remain some personal vision, the business equivalent of a daydream. You also have failed to remember leadership is a partnership, that you're all in the boat together and when adversity hits you're all going to be in the life preserver together.

Don't fail to remember that your success is intricately linked to the people you are leading and you can't be successful unless they are. You must also realize that things are going to fluctuate, almost like a stock price, up and down. So you have to get back to your fundamentals and ride out the tough times until you start to rise again. You have to also be aware of those around you and know that you might very well have to count on them for your job.

Reading the Vince Lombardi book—*When Pride Still Mattered* by David Maraniss—made me examine my weaknesses more.

Lombardi always has been a mythic figure to me, the person I admired most in coaching. That began when I was in college and first started to read about Lombardi, the legendary coach of the Green Bay Packers in the 1960s. I had seen one of those *NFL Flashbacks* on Lombardi and also had seen the movie with Ernest Borgnine, and I became fascinated with both Lombardi and his methods. I read everything I could about him. I was fascinated by the way he spoke, the way he used his voice to command respect, the way he demanded things.

Lombardi was one of the greatest coaches in history, the man who led the Packers to the top of the NFL. He also understood the power of motivation and was able to translate that to the players he coached. He had a way of taking a disparate group of individuals and, through his will, mold them into people that were willing to lay it all on the line for the team.

I remember reading a quote by him years ago, one I've never forgotten: "Individual commitment to a group effort," he said. "That's what makes a team work, a company work, a society work, a civilization work."

So much of what I've come to believe is in that quotation.

The other thing I always admired about Lombardi was the way he balanced discipline and love. He believed you had to have both, the discipline to establish the group's structure, and the love to make everyone help one another. No one had a better mixture of discipline and love than Lombardi.

There's a part in the book when he talks about how anyone can love somebody's strengths and somebody's good looks. But can you accept someone for his inabilities? He didn't want his players picking on one another, but rather concentrating on what they could do to make it easier on the rest of their teammates. Lombardi always understood that.

He also understood the basic concepts of motivation, namely that everyone can't be motivated the same way. Lombardi knew his players. He knew who had to be prodded and who had to be pulled, who he could yell at and who he couldn't. He knew his players' individual buttons. In so many ways Lombardi was a coaching genius.

But Lombardi was not the saint I always had made him out to be. He always said that the great trilogy in his life was "God, Family, Packers," but he didn't treat his family well. He never forgave Jim Taylor for leaving the Packers, even though he later coached a year with the Redskins. He belittled everyone from Monday through Thursday. The love was only there on Friday and Saturday.

I also used to think Lombardi could have coached in any era, but after reading *When Pride Still Mattered* I now don't think so. Lombardi could not have dealt with the current media, certainly not in the way he did when he coached. He held grudges. He denied writers with whom he was feuding access to the team. He tried to control his environment in ways you simply can't do today. In short, he had flaws.

Just as all leaders have flaws.

Take Bill Parcells, for example. Especially how he responded when his New York Jets lost the AFC Championship game to the Denver Broncos in January of 1999. Now Parcells is a great football coach, a widely praised leader. He's been called the best football coach since Lombardi, a modern day Lombardi, and I would certainly agree.

But what did he say after his team lost, a game in which they had several damaging turnovers?

He was upset that his players had lost their fundamentals in such a big game.

After watching a *60 Minutes* profile on him, I saw that the Lombardi-Parcells comparison is right on the money. Both men are driven, passionate, expect nothing less than a winning effort, and will be long remembered for their coaching brilliance. What I walked away with, though,—as a current coach—is that for all their brilliance, for all their victories, it just doesn't seem as if they enjoyed it enough. That's not a knock, for my admiration for both men couldn't be higher. But it's a lesson for all of us: we must enjoy what we're doing.

But back to Parcells's reaction after losing that playoff game in 1999.

I did a similar thing when, at Kentucky, we lost to North Carolina one year in a regional final. At the time, it was a devastating loss, for we did not play well, nor did we play smart, and those are the kind of games that haunt you when you're a coach, especially when the stakes are so high. These are the things I talked about in the interview room after the game. What I should have been doing was praising North Carolina. But I had been too wrapped up in my own disappointment. Looking at what both Parcells and I did, the lesson is that the best way to deal with a defeat is to praise the opposition.

There's a lesson to be learned in this: No matter how great the leader there are always human frailties and these frailties eventually come out, especially in times of stress. There is no perfection among leaders.

My greatest failings as a leader, though, have come when I've lost my temper.

These are moments when I have lost control and when you lose control you both say things and do things that you often don't mean. Invariably, when this happens these things will come back to haunt you. When you can't control your emotions you can cause harm, for those kind of eruptions are harmful to a group. Don't misunderstand. You can erupt. You can have moments when you're angry and you can let that anger show. These times can be motivating, but you can't let yourself lose control of your emotions.

As a leader you must discipline your emotions.

My other great failing as a leader was I tended to dominate things too much. My first year with the Celtics we didn't get enough accomplished in staff meetings because I dominated the meetings too much. I had gotten away from what I believe is the principle rule about good communication—that you should listen about four times more than you speak.

That's why leaders need introspection.

You must recognize your flaws.

Knowing yourself—your strengths, weaknesses, and your values—is essential, as is being able to ask yourself difficult questions. Are you being true to your values? Is everything still headed toward the future? Have you forgotten what made you successful in the first place? Are you thinking selfishly or about the team? Have you embraced success?

You must always be asking yourself these questions.

DON'T COMPETE WITH THOSE YOU LEAD

You must always be using your power to help people.

That might sound like an obvious statement, but it really isn't.

It's easy to take advantage of any leadership position, whether by accepting the perks that come with the job, expecting people to treat you deferentially, or simply by abusing your power.

My former assistants are always telling stories about how difficult it was to work for me. All the long hours they put in, all the crazy things they had to do. It's as if they're all members of some private club and these stories are part of the initiation night, so there's always an element of "can you top this?" These stories are told with great humor and like all stories, they get exaggerated over the course of time, but whenever I hear them a little bell goes off in my head, too. For I did work them hard. I did sometimes make them do crazy things. There were ways I treated them I regret now.

For you must treat your assistants with respect, too.

You can't misuse your power. You can't abuse it. You must always be using your power to help people.

In a sense you must always have your own checkpoints, your own little system of checks and balances. What are your goals? Are you being true to your values? Are you still moving toward your vision? Because it's so easy to stray, especially the more successful you become.

It's almost become a cliché. You hear this all the time, about the people who become very successful only to forget where they came from, forget their roots. In a sense, it's one of the worst things you can say about people and you must be forever vigilant that it doesn't happen to you.

Because it's easy to lose your way.

Just as it's easy for people in the workplace to lose focus, it's also easy for leaders to forget their core values, drift from their vision. You must never lose sight of why you have power in the first place, the inherent premise that comes with any kind of leadership situation; namely, that you're supposed to be helping people to become more successful.

In coaching, it's often called putting players in positions where they can be successful. That's a microcosm for any kind of leadership. You can't be competing with people. You can't be threatened by their achievements. You can't be hoping they're going to stay in the same positions forever. You must rejoice in their successes, wish them well when they outgrow you and move on, just as parents do when their children grow up and leave the house to go off on their own.

BE OF SERVICE

When I first got to Kentucky I didn't realize what I represented, the fact that Kentucky basketball is so ingrained in the state, how important it was to so many people, both emotionally and psychologically. In my mind, I always had been just a basketball coach.

It didn't take me long, however, to realize I was the caretaker of all this and that it was something to watch over very carefully. It wasn't about me; it was about what I represented. Coaches come and go, but the tradition of Kentucky basketball remains forever.

That realization had two sides to it:

Because of the power of the position it was very easy to get things accomplished. In just two months we raised enough money to start a shelter for the homeless in Owensboro, Kentucky, that's named for my son Daniel, who died when he was six months old of a congenital heart defect. It feeds a hundred people a day and has beds for sixty.

The flip side was the responsibility that came with that, the very real sense that being the head of Kentucky basketball had very little to do with me and everything to do with what this basketball program meant to the state of Kentucky, the people of Kentucky. It was very humbling and it was one of the messages I was always giving to my players at Kentucky—they weren't just playing for themselves or their teammates or even their university. They were playing for all those people who had never been inside Rupp Arena in Lexington but who had spent so much of their lives caring about Kentucky basketball, giving their hearts to it. They were playing for all the people who felt better about themselves when Kentucky won, all those people who were emotionally connected to it in ways that people who weren't from Kentucky couldn't understand. They were playing for all the players who had come before, the ones who had built the tradition, the ones who had expanded upon it. And they were playing for all the players who would come after them, would come after me. That was always my message to them, that they were all part of this continuum that was Kentucky basketball, this wonderful tapestry that was full of so many different threads.

This was what we had to protect. This was the heirloom we had to keep polishing.

And when you begin to look at things this way it's almost impossible to be selfish, to be self-oriented. When you realize you're a part of something that's far greater than yourself it's easier to subordinate your own self-interest.

That's the ideal, what you are always striving for.

From your first meeting when you present the vision, through all the traits of leadership, what you are striving for is selflessness: the selflessness of the individual members of the group, the selflessness of the leader. The sense that the whole is greater than the sum of the individual parts. That's the essence of what all great groups have, the one common denominator. They become families in the very best sense of the world, people who care for one another, who help one another.

One day, shortly into the 1999–2000 season, the weekly poll question in the *Boston Herald* asked if I should be fired as the coach of the Celtics. Someone left the article on my desk and my first reaction was why would someone do that?

But you know what my second reaction was?

What would Tim Sypher—who gave up a job three years ago to come work for me—do if I were fired? What would happen to John Connor, our equipment man who quit his previous job to come work for me when I got the Celtics job? What would happen to my assistant coaches, my staff? What would happen to the people who had hitched their fate to mine, the people who were now dependent on me?

That's when I knew I had truly evolved as a leader.

Because when I was younger my first reaction undoubtedly would have been a personal one. What would I do now? How would this affect my career, my family? Where would I go next? The inevitable personal questions. Now, though, my first reaction was to be concerned with everyone else, not just myself.

That's what leaders do.

They concern themselves with the well-being of others.

I am asked all the time whether winning the national championship at Kentucky in the spring of 1996 was the high point of my career. Certainly, it was one of them. It was one of those nights when you remember all the things you do early in your career, all the dues paying, all those years when you were so far from ever winning anything like a national championship, all those years when winning a national championship is as far away as Oz.

All those memories came rushing at me that night, like some newsreel in my head I couldn't stop. All the recruiting visits when I was at Boston University in search of kids I knew I'd never get. All the coaching at summer camps when I was just starting out. All the speaking at summer camps when I was try-ing to make a name for myself. All the traveling and hours spent away from my family. All the cramped locker rooms and cold gyms. All the miles you travel when you are just beginning on the road, just trying to survive in the game.

I remembered all those things that night, how very far I had come since I was just a little kid falling in love with a game, a game that has come to define so much of my life. Could anyone have asked for more? That night in the Meadowlands, seeing us win the national championship, I didn't think so.

But while it certainly was one of the most wonderful mo-ments in my life, something I will cherish forever—not only for it being the symbolic top of the mountain in my profession but also because of the tremendous joy it gave to everyone in the state of Kentucky—in all honesty the night of the NBA draft in 1996, that was three months later, where I saw four of my play-ers get drafted was just as sweet.

I saw those four young men, who had worked so hard, hug-ging their families. I knew how much getting drafted meant to them. I knew how much it meant to their families. I knew how very far they had come from when they had first arrived at Ken-tucky as freshmen, full of the same doubts and uncertainties all freshmen have when they enter college. I knew how hard they had worked as players, how much they had to surrender some of their individual goals for the sake of the team. I knew how much they had sacrificed and now I saw them being rewarded for it, all their basketball dreams coming true.

That was the ultimate moment in my career.

I got more satisfaction that night than from any individual awards I've ever won. Because I knew I had played a role in some-thing that was filling someone else's cup with so much joy.

Because what you eventually find out when you're looking for your own gratification is that it's essentially short-lived. Yes, it's nice to win awards and be recognized for your accomplish-ments, yet those, ultimately, have a very short shelf life. But when you've had a hand in someone else's success that connection, that bond, can last a lifetime.

That is the essence of leadership.

That is what makes the job worthwhile.

That is what makes success continually worth striving for.

KEY CHAPTER POINTS

● **Own Up to Your Flaws** It is not enough to simply be good at what you do. Your vision can't be a personal one. It must be one you can transform to others. We all have flaws, but it's important that you recognize what they are. You must always be asking yourself difficult questions: Are you being true to your values? Is everything still geared toward the future?

● **Don't Compete with Those You Lead** You must always be using your power to help people. You can't be competing with people you are leading, but doing everything you can to make their situation better.

● **Be of Service** The true leader is a selfless leader. Everything you do as a leader must be geared to nurturing an environment that makes people's lives better.

RICHARD LAPCHICK

Few leaders in any capacity are more admired, honored, or universally respected than Richard Lapchick. His is a voice that is sought out—and heard—by many of the world's most influential figures, especially those working to help better race relations in this country and around the world. Nelson Mandela, Martin Luther King Jr., Jimmy Carter, Jesse Jackson, Muhammad Ali, and Arthur Ashe are among those he has worked with in this capacity over the years.

But that's only the tip of the iceberg. As founder and director of the Center for the Study of Sport in Society at Northeastern University, Richard has been a pioneer in several areas—ensuring the education of athletes from junior high through the professional ranks, and advocating violence prevention. The center's Project TEAMWORK was called "America's most successful violence prevention program," while its MVP gender violence prevention program was such a success at the high school and college levels that the United States Marines adopted it in 1997.

The center helped form the National Consortium for Academics and Sports, which now includes more than 179 colleges and universities. Because of their efforts, more than 13,000 athletes have returned to school and nearly half of them have graduated.

For more than twenty years, Richard was the American leader of the international campaign to boycott sports in South Africa. In 1993, the center launched TEAMWORK–South Africa, a program designed to use sports as a way to improve race relations and help with sports development in post-apartheid South Africa. In recognition and appreciation of his efforts, Richard was one of two hundred guests specially invited by Mandela to attend his inauguration.

The range of honors bestowed upon Richard is remarkable. The Ralph Bunche International Peace Award, the Arthur Ashe Voice of Conscience Award, and the Women's Sports Foundation President's Award are but a few. For six consecutive years (1993–'98), Richard was included among the hundred most powerful people in sports. Even more important, he was described as '"the racial conscience of sport."

Richard grew up in an environment that provided him with a keen awareness of the importance of racial harmony. His father, Joe Lapchick, was a legendary figure in the world of sports, spending nearly fifty years in a Hall of Fame career as a basketball player and coach. It was in those gyms and arenas that young Richard observed his father blending together black and white players for a common cause. The primary lesson Richard learned was that harmony leads to victory, while friction can only end in failure.

"My father was a great leader who just happened to be a coach," Richard says. "For me, a great leader is someone who has the quality that can inspire people to perform at their highest level and to achieve whatever the goal of the team or individual may be. My father had that quality."

And so have many others that Richard has worked with and advised over the years. What he has learned is that beneath their differences lie common threads that unite all of them.

"Great leaders come from all walks of life and have very different personalities," Richard says. "However, in my experience, I've found that all successful leaders share several common traits. Being able to listen is a key factor. A good leader must be able to hear people, to sense what they need. A good leader must get the respect of the people very quickly so that little time is spent questioning him or her.

"The good leader must somehow manage to instill confidence into those under him that he's going to do what's best for the organization. Then the leader must be willing to listen to what's being said. He must be unafraid to seek out opinions, to be challenged. That helps bring people on board. The leader must also make sure that negative people know they must either become part of the team or leave the team."

In addition to being fearless, Richard says a good leader must also be willing to admit mistakes.

"Arthur Ashe was a good friend and a man I greatly admired," Richard said. "Arthur helped me understand how to say, 'I was wrong.' Arthur went against the boycott and played tennis in South Africa. It was a decision he later came to regret. And he was man enough to admit that he'd been wrong. It takes courage to do that."

Richard acknowledges that the leader's role has changed over the years. Gone are the days when an iron-fisted leader could rule with absolute authority. Today's leader, Richard says, faces a much more difficult and complex situation: Be firm, yet also understanding.

"Today, there is a much greater expectation from talented people that a leader will take them under their wing and mentor them," Richard says. "Many young people today are aggressively seeking that mentorship. Being a mentor has now almost become part of a leader's job description."

But what about compromise? When must a leader be willing to bend? Or should he?

"That depends on the issue," Richard says. "Of course, there are situations when every leader must be willing to compromise. However, on some big issues, you should never compromise your core beliefs. You must always keep in mind that you can lose a battle and still win the war. Focus on the core element and then build a coalition that can be successful."

The great leaders, the ones who make a difference, regardless of the time in which they lived, never allow fame or fortune to stand in the way of achieving their desired goals.

"I've spent time with King, [Cesar] Chavez, Mandela," Richard says. "They were all great leaders. I also think Mikhail Gorbachev will go down as one of the truly great leaders of this century. Jimmy Carter, as well. One thing that really struck me about all these great leaders was their humility. They were very humble. They never touted their own greatness. They just *were* great. Even Muhammad Ali, who was anything but humble as a young man, has found a quiet dignity in silence."

EPILOGUE

Leadership is always evolving.

It's never static. It's always changing, just as your group or organization is always changing. No situation ever stays the same. There always are new challenges, as well as the ongoing ones we face every day. That's a lesson that was reinforced for me midway through the 1999–2000 season, in my third year with the Celtics.

We were going through a difficult stretch approaching the All-Star break, the symbolic halfway point of the season, and I was beginning to see the look of defeat. Invariably, we would be very competitive for most of the game, then start to fall behind in the fourth quarter. I could see it in the players' eyes as they came to the bench during a timeout. It was that look of defeat. They were deflating right in front of me. They were succumbing to a sense of failure.

And you can't do that.

In our last practice before the All-Star break, I posed this question: Who is willing to go to war? I told them that it's not enough that you feel badly when you lose. This keeps you in a cycle of despair and inaction. The question is, are you willing to pay the price to turn things around?

Earlier that day, I had a conversation with Antoine Walker.

I told him that this was now his fourth year with the Boston Celtics, and it might also be the fourth year he's not been in the playoffs. I told him that he will take the blame for that, just as I and the rest of his teammates will. I told him that I thought he was beginning to let the losing get to him, and if that was the case, then maybe he should look into going to another team for a fresh start.

"No," he told me. "I want to stay with the Celtics."

Then you can't succumb to losing," I said. "You must battle losing."

Just as I had to battle it.

I told Antoine that we were coming close in games. We were more competitive than we'd been in the past, but we weren't winning. At night, I would go home and play the game tapes over and over. Each game seemed like the same tape. I told him that this was the hardest thing I had ever gone through in my professional life. I was working harder than I had when I was a young coach, yet nothing seemed to be enough. The team was so young, so poor defensively.

But my message—both to Antoine and the rest of the players—was that we are all in the foxhole together and that we will crawl out of it if we don't get cynical, don't start pointing fingers, and don't get beaten down by losing.

We were about to go on a six-game road trip out West, the kind of trip that never had been kind to the Celtics in the past. So, I challenged the players, essentially telling them that we had to go to work and stop complaining. We had to learn to stop deflating. We had to have heart and courage and resolve to stay the course.

In a sense, we had to live in a future of hope and success, and not dwell on a past that would get us down.

And what do you do as a leader?

You deflate behind closed doors.

I have a lot of bad nights. I have a lot of times when I'm down. But when I get up in the morning, I'm upbeat, positive, and have a plan for the future. For the thing I have learned in the NBA is that there are no Cinderella stories.

It's true that I've been a part of a lot of Cinderella stories over the years in college ball, but this is the heavyweight division of basketball, and it's about talent. The job is about acquiring and developing talent, and that takes time. It can't be expedited. It's one thing to go from 15 wins to 36 wins like we did in my first year with the Celtics. A lot of that you could do with hard work and effort. But going from 36 wins to 46 wins is about talent.

What gives me inspiration is looking at other leaders who have gone through great periods of adversity, but who persevered and triumphed in the end.

I see someone like Joe Torre, the manager of the New York Yankees, who just won back-to-back World Series. If you look at Torre now, he seems the personification of the perfect leader. He deals with superstar players who make millions of dollars. He deals with the most difficult media in the country. He deals with a difficult owner. He dealt with adversity in his family, the well-publicized illness of his brother Frank. He dealt with his own prostate cancer. Through it all, he retained both grace and class.

Yet, if you look at his record prior to his coming to the Yankees, it was below .500. He had managed the Braves, Mets, and Cardinals, and in many ways had been a victim of circumstance. What Torre did, however, was to keep believing in himself and his methods. He kept believing that he was a good enough Major League manager to win a world championship if he was in the right situation. Through all of his tough times, he kept believing that even if he might not be able to win as much as he wanted, he could still be successful. For Torre always believed that success was getting the most out of his potential, both personally and professionally.

That's a great lesson for all of us.

You can't deflate when things aren't moving as quickly as you want them to. You can't get down, especially as a leader. Because if you deflate in public, then everyone around you will immediately deflate, too. You cannot lose your optimism. I look at my situation here with the Celtics, at this difficult task of rebuilding this proud franchise, and I know I cannot lose my optimism; I am never going to lose that. I am going to be optimistic at every job I ever have, and I am going to believe in a better future for everyone. I can't stop raising the bar, for that's what leaders do. They keep pushing the people they are leading.

You have to stick to it. And that's not just basketball or business. That's life, too.